Interpreting the Old Testament

INTERPRETING THE
OLD TESTAMENT

———◆———

FRITZ STOLZ

SCM PRESS LTD

Translated by Margaret Kohl from the German
Das Alte Testament
first published 1974
by Gütersloher Verlagshaus Gerd Mohn, Gütersloh

334 00668 6
First British edition 1975
published by SCM Press Ltd
58 Bloomsbury Street London

© SCM Press Ltd 1975
Printed in Great Britain by
Northumberland Press Limited
Gateshead

Contents

Introduction

The aim

Scholarly work on the Old Testament seems to be a somewhat confusing mass of possible interpretations, hypotheses and dogmatic assertions. This wide range of opinion is largely due to the fact that particular scholars approach their material with different presuppositions and different questions in mind. It is not as if the problems inherent in particular material were fixed right from the outset; the answers depend on the particular perspective from which a subject is approached.

It follows from this that attention should always be paid to the particular question which prompts an exegetical statement. This requirement might seem obvious, but in fact it is often evident that statements and opinions are compared which differ so widely from one another in terms of the kind of questions they raise that they cannot be directly compared, even if they relate to the same material.

Critical assessments of exegetical statements are therefore bound to follow up and examine the whole course of the argument from initial question to final result. Special attention should be paid to this methodological background of the process of interpretation whenever it is not explicitly stated – as is generally the case, since in the course of his work a scholar arrives at a more or less 'normal' pattern of methodological procedure which he does not always make clear on every occasion.

Thus it is all the more important for anyone who is not professionally concerned with the interpretation of the Old Testament to be familiar with the basic questions with which the exegesis of the Old Testament is occupied. Once a reader has succeeded in understanding the methods used in specialist literature, taking into account the starting point of an exegetical judgment and the scope of the question behind it, he can then arrive at an independent judgment, and into this judgment he will also be able to incorporate his own intellectual position. I hope that this book will help in this respect.

Some theological starting points

On the whole, the exegetical questions asked today have grown up since the Enlightenment. Within this period historical-critical research did its pioneer work; that is to say, after the Enlightenment the biblical texts were no longer viewed as applying directly to the present, but were supposed to be read in their historical context, with critical detachment.

However, detachment does not mean that the exegete approaches his text without any presuppositions at all. Every period has its own way of formulating its own particular problems, and it is obvious that every interpreter will come to a text with the questions of his own period in mind: explicitly or implicitly, consciously or unconsciously. For when all is said and done, in dealing with the biblical texts he is ultimately seeking directions for his *own* time and a clarification of his own situation. Since the Enlightenment, the points of reference and the interests of exegetical questions have altered time and again. They must be viewed in close connection with the general history of ideas and theology; the exegetical work of every generation reflects the current problems which have to be met in that particular period.

Now the different questions raised did not, of course, simply follow one after the other; they were also superimposed on each other and exercised influence simultaneously, sometimes in rivalry, sometimes as mutually supplementary explanations. The results of research often continued to exert an influence even after new interests had already led to investigations and hypotheses of a different kind.

As a result, Old Testament exegesis today is trustee over a richly varied heritage of questions, methodological approaches and results, which have their origin in theological interests which differ in each given case. Different questions do not necessarily exclude one another; the latest accounts of methods of interpreting the Old Testament show well how one method can supplement another, building up a comprehensive survey which can illuminate the various aspects of a text. In certain circumstances, however, different methodological approaches can become rivals; in that case it is necessary to consider carefully the interests that lie behind an approach to the text, the methodological differences which result, and the way in which the text itself exerts an influence – or perhaps a corrective influence – on the method employed. In order to deal adequately with the methods, then, we need insight into their background in the history of theology. The more distant a particular theological era, the easier it is to acquire this insight. In the following chapters we shall be outlining three periods which have proved to be pioneering for developments in Old Testament exegesis: the nineteenth century, with its questions about the Old Testament writers and their works; the beginning of the twentieth century, with its interest in the community and its part in the growth of literature; and the period following the First World War, with its theological reflections on the true nature of the church and of faith and the exegetical concerns resulting from these reflections. In a fourth section we shall indicate starting points for the systematic use of the Old Testament; here the historical approach must inevitably recede into the background, but it should nevertheless be clear how exegetical questionings and results are incorporated in systematic reflections.

It is obvious that the questions which particularly typify our contemporary life cannot be reduced to a single common denominator. In the actual process of interpretation, new groups of problems constantly come into play (one need only think of structuralist literary criticism or interpretation based on depth psychology – there are already many examples of both). Only the future can show which of these can gain a permanent footing and become an established method.

How to use this book

The chapters which have been shaped by the history of theology start by giving an account of the essential cultural and theological

impulses and the pioneering theologians who represent them. It
will then be evident how this kind of questioning was applied to the
Old Testament material, which results came to fruition and which
methodological procedures became established. Of course, the account can be no more than a series of examples; at the end of the
book the reader will find details of textbooks which have contributed
to the present work and which may be of use in further reading.

I

The Old Testament Writers

1. The Background

Understanding scripture before the Enlightenment

For centuries the Old Testament was read and interpreted in a different way from the other works of world literature; it counted as being fundamentally different from other books, and therefore as demanding special treatment and attention. Its author was held to be the Holy Spirit (the doctrine of inspiration); human writers were thought to be merely the instruments of the Spirit. The doctrine of inspiration was certainly not given the same weight at all times and in all places – for example there was a dispute within Reformed orthodoxy over the extent of inspiration: whether it was confined to the Hebrew consonants or also extended to the vowels supplied later by the Massoretes. The Reformers themselves seem to have acted remarkably freely in contrast to more rigid and formal doctrines of inspiration. However, their hesitations about biblical texts were not prompted by recognition of the historical relativity and limitations of the biblical writers. Their criticism was criticism of content, which was founded on central theological judgments. The criterion by which the Reformers judged the individual writings was: to what degree were they expressions of the work of Christ, either plainly or in hidden form? The question about the human character and historical limitations of the authors of the individual writings did not come to the fore until modern times.

The claims of reason

With the Enlightenment the situation altered fundamentally. The

Enlightenment made it possible for men – even theologians! – to base their thinking on autonomous human reason instead of on revelation. It was never doubted that reason was unanimous and unambiguous – and direct divine authority was claimed for it. Consequently, a critical detachment to holy scripture became possible. It was no longer taken to be God's direct word; authority had to be able to stand the test of rational examination. In this detached way of observation it was now possible to ask about the man who composed a biblical writing – about his particular way of expressing the divine revelation. It was also possible to ask whether he illuminated it or obscured it.

This is only a brief summary of a tendency which began to emerge among certain scholars from the seventeenth century onwards and which increasingly gained ground as time went on. Contradictory tendencies ran parallel to it; for example, there was a type of orthodoxy which sought a clearer intellectual grasp of the process of inspiration (though in so doing it also recognized in its own way the claim of reason). In the period after the Enlightenment, most interpreters tried to do justice to different trends and to satisfy the claims of reason and revelation alike. Of course this was bound to lead to inconsistencies. Accordingly, it was also a very long time before the biblical writers could really be viewed as human authors.

Interest in the Pentateuch

For various reasons, at the beginning of historical-critical research interest was first fired by the five books of Moses. On the one hand, from Judaism onwards the Torah had generally been accepted as the central section of the Old Testament canon. On the other hand, the period of the Enlightenment, with its keen ethical interest, paid particular attention to the legal parts of the Old Testament. As the normative Old Testament authority, Moses therefore became a centre of attention from a number of different perspectives. Finally, the very books which were traditionally assigned to Moses presented particular difficulties for the understanding. From the seventeenth century onwards there were discussions as to whether Moses was really the author of the Pentateuch; whether one could reckon with a single author at all; whether at any rate Moses might have based his work on a number of different sources, which would explain the contradictions in his writings, and so on.

Understanding the Pentateuch: problems and attempted solutions

There are various difficulties in understanding the Pentateuch as the consistent work of one writer. Several stories with the same theme appear twice or even three times: the best-known examples are the story of the creation, which appears twice in immediate succession (Gen. 1.1ff. and 2.4bff.), and the story of the peril of the mother of the race which is told three times (Gen. 12.10ff.; 20; 26.7-11). There are often peculiar repetitions even within individual stories. Where the same stories, or parts of them, occur twice or three times, they are called *doublets*.

There are many tensions and contradictions in the content of the Pentateuch. For instance, we have three different names for Moses' father-in-law (Hobab, Reuel and Jethro). The contradictions often appear in doublets (e.g. in the story of the flood Noah is to take seven pairs of every clean animal and one pair of every unclean animal into the ark according to Gen. 7.2; according to Gen. 7.8 it was one pair of each kind, clean and unclean alike).

A few sections of the Pentateuch (e.g. Ex. 17.14) purport to have been written by Moses himself; in other places (e.g. Gen. 36.1), the text presupposes an Israelite monarchy, which of course points to a much later period.

In the course of time more and more scholars gave up assuming that Moses was the author of the Pentateuch. Various hypotheses were suggested in an attempt to solve the difficulties of understanding.

(a) The documentary hypothesis. This theory presupposes the existence of different literary works of considerable size which were ultimately worked together into a coherent whole. It postulates two active roles, first the author of an original work ('written source' or 'narrative strand') and secondly a 'redactor'. The redactor makes use of the written sources and destroys their coherence; he either uses individual blocks of the source narrative as bricks in the

coherent pattern which he wants to create, or he atomizes the stories completely, combining tiny units together. Now and again he has to create bridge passages, etc., and here redactional passages are to be found.

(b) The fragment hypothesis. This starts from the assumption that there were originally a large number of single stories ('fragments'). It then assumes a collector who arranged the fragments, or at least combined them to form a narrative whole.

(c) The supplementary hypothesis combines the two preceding hypotheses. A story is in existence; a redactor (or several redactors) first inserts individual 'fragments' into the narrative whole; the disturbances to be observed in the text can be explained in this way.

Hardly ever has a single one of these theories been used to explain the entire Pentateuch. The various sections have suggested now one and now another; and the more imaginative interpreters recognized that a mechanical application of one hypothetical pattern does not do justice to the texts.

The attempts to discover the original literary units and the efforts to explain the genesis of the present text (which has often been damaged) were given the name literary criticism (see further pp. 56ff. below).

Literary criticism and the history of Israel

Interest in the history of Israel developed simultaneously with the work of literary criticism. The critical analysis of the writings of the Pentateuch (and of the other Old Testament books) was to contribute to knowledge of the true history of Israel, the aim here being not only the reconstruction of historical facts but also an understanding of the inner development of the Israelite spirit and Israelite religion.

The different outlines given to a 'history of Israel' are closely bound up with the general understanding of history in the period of the Enlightenment. In broad terms, two tendencies can be indicated between which there is a certain opposition. The anthropological optimism of the period of the Enlightenment sprang from a belief in progress, the expectation of a steady moral and intellectual perfecting of man. A historical picture tending towards perfection appears in a totally different form in Idealism, which is concerned with progress in the realm of the spirit through a consciousness of freedom.

On the other hand, a movement also developed directed against the Enlightenment. One particularly clear example in the eighteenth century is Jean-Jacques Rousseau, but the movement also became influential later in Romanticism. Here man's natural origins are seen as an ideal state, whereas the development of civilization is thought to lead in the wrong direction. The initial stages of civilizations, in the freshness of their powers, become the norm for judging historical phenomena.

The two trends which have been broadly outlined are not necessarily mutually exclusive. They often combined to stimulate particular writers and thinkers. The same is true in the case of the outlines of the history of Israel which were developed by Old Testament scholars in the nineteenth century. This is particularly clear in the case of Julius Wellhausen.

Julius Wellhausen

Wellhausen (1844-1918) was the supreme embodiment of nineteenth-century effort in literary criticism; his work pointed the way for the interpreters who came after him. At first Professor of Old Testament studies at Greifswald, his scholarly activity caused so much commotion among church members that he felt that if anything he was disqualifying theological students from their profession. Consequently he left the theological faculty and turned to Arabic studies. His evaluation of Old Testament phenomena as well as his work on literary criticism and the history of Israel continue even now to have their effect. Two works are conveniently accessible in English translation, the *Prolegomena to the History of Israel* (1883, ET 1885, reprinted 1957) and an article on the history of Israel which appeared in the *Encyclopaedia Britannica* of 1881 and was reprinted as an appendix to the ET of the *Prolegomena*; since some of the phraseology is echoed in Wellhausen's later *Israelitische und jüdische Geschichte* of 1894, phrases have been incorporated where appropriate in the translation of passages from the *Geschichte* quoted below. Wellhausen's third major work on the Old Testament was *Die Composition des Hexateuchs* of 1885. The three titles are referred to below in abbreviated form.

(a) From Pentateuchal criticism to the history of Israel. The basic features of the way in which Wellhausen clarifies the problems of literary criticism raised by the Pentateuch in CH are still largely recognized as being correct. Wellhausen prefers the documentary hypothesis. The basis of the Pentateuch is the latest of the source documents, Q (from *quattuor*, representing the 'Book of four covenants'; today the symbol P, for 'Priestly writing', is used for this source). Q is preserved in its entirety, but has been supplemented by a work (JE = Jehovist) compiled from two sources (J = Jahwist; E = Elohist). The work is concluded with D (Deuteronomy). The chronological development of the Pentateuch therefore took the following form. J and E came into being in the middle of the monarchy, they were fused together by a redactor into JE. D was composed shortly before the exile. Finally, Q is post-exilic in origin, although it now forms the literary foundation of the whole work in its edited form. The individual insights which made this literary-critical classification possible were not Wellhausen's own achievement. However, it was reserved for him to sum up the observations of previous interpreters in one single, convincing outline.

These insights were now put at the service of a historical concept. In his *Prolegomena* Wellhausen first investigates the history of the Israelite cult, which he deduces primarily from legal texts. The five main cultic themes (the place of worship, sacrifice, the sacred feasts, the priests and levites, priestly equipment) are marked in Wellhausen's account by a unified development which can be traced to the stages JE – D – P. In the first stage (JE) the multiplicity of the cult and its direct links with nature are marked: the cult is interwoven with everyday life; it is a matter for every family and accompanies normal, natural life at every step. In this way it is completely rooted in the peasant-farming life of early Israel.

The second stage, D, brings a radical alteration to this under-standing of the cult. The cult is now confined to what takes place in the sanctuary in Jerusalem; this is the sole legitimate place of worship and here alone may sacrifices be made by the priests appointed for the task. The basis of the feasts in nature is supple-mented by a historical foundation.

At the third stage, P, the cult is completely 'denaturalized': the original direct link with nature is completely abandoned. The ritual takes on significance in itself and is not a reflection of living reality; real life is smothered in ritual regulations. Wellhausen goes on to show that there was a similar development in the narrative parts of the Old Testament.

(b) The beginnings of the history of Israel. In *IJG* Wellhausen spoke of Israel's beginnings in characteristic terms:

'At the time of Moses the people of Israel grew up out of a situation of necessity – grew up out of related peoples and tribes, and elevated itself above them. The new unity was hallowed by Jehovah, who it is true existed earlier, but who now for the first time took his place at the head of this people. Jehovah is the God of Israel, and Israel is the people of Jehovah; that is the beginning and the enduring principle of the political and religious history that follows ... Israel's life was Jehovah's life. The pre-eminent expression of the nation's life was then and for centuries afterwards war' (pp. 25f.). 'The camp, the cradle of the nation, was also its primitive sanctuary. There Israel was, and there was Jehovah' (p. 27).

Cultic activity, too, had its origin here, special religious com-mandments regulating Israel's dealings with its God in battle.

The sense of community which strengthened the Israelites above all in battle also took concrete form in a peaceful common life; a strong sense of justice arose which took its bearings from Yahweh. The law of Yahweh was proclaimed in particular by the seer-priests, one of whom was Moses. It was therefore a living law, not a rigid system of commandments.

Wellhausen called this Israelite form of life 'theocracy': Yahweh's rule manifesting itself directly through help in war and legislation. It was an era in which 'war and the administration of justice were regarded as matters of religion before they became matters of obligation and civil order' (p. 30).

(c) Wellhausen's appraisal of Israelite history. Wellhausen's sympathy – perhaps enthusiasm might be a better word – becomes noticeable wherever the 'original character' of a historical phenomenon can be grasped. The nature of this originality is not so important. In the *Prolegomena* he finds the 'originality' in the nature-bound cult of the pre-exilic period, in which agricultural life and ritual celebration are directly bound up together; in *IJG* the originality is to be found in the direct experience of divine leadership in war and in the rise of the nation connected with it.

Prophecy is also essential for Wellhausen's evaluation of Israel's history. It introduced a development going beyond theocracy. During the period of the monarchy, syncretism between Yahweh and the Canaanite fertility-god Baal became a matter of course for the broad masses of the Israelite people. At this point the prophetic protest intervenes: Elijah, the first clearly recognizable prophet, finds it intolerable that Yahweh the God of Israel and Baal the god of fertility should be revered in the same way.

'This prophet towers alone above his time; only saga could preserve his image, not history. One has the indefinite impression that with him the idea of Jehovah entered on a new phase, yet it is hardly possible to decide wherein the difference from earlier times consists. Jehovah was first of all active in the political sector, and had founded the nation and the empire; now in the spiritual sphere he reacted against the foreign elements which had up to then been able to gain access almost unhindered ... Elijah grasped Jehovah as a principle full of meaning, which was incapable of being reconciled with Baal in one and the same breast. To Elijah it was apparent for the first time that different areas of life do not own different forces, worthy of adoration, but that there is everywhere but one Holy and Mighty Power which reveals itself, not in nature, but in the law and justice of the world of man' (*Grundrisse zum Alten Testament*, articles edited by R. Smend, 1965, p. 38). Admittedly, 'Elijah ascended to heaven without having achieved very much on earth' (ibid.).

Here we seem to have the beginning of a rift in ancient Israel: on the one hand the people with its cult-bound religiosity; on the other the prophet, who elevates the bond with Yahweh into the realm of the spirit. How are we to judge this rift?

Although in truth the Torah and the moral influence of Jehovah on life was something far more important and far more truly Israelite than the cult, yet the cult was in general more highly valued by common opinion. For the common man it was liturgical, not moral behaviour, that counted as being truly religious ... The cult no longer possessed its old simplicity; at the great sanctuaries in particular – Bethel, Gilgal, Beersheba – it had become opulent to a degree (ibid., pp. 43f.).

The cult which the prophets reject is therefore no longer the simple, primeval celebration of natural life; it is its exalted caricature. Thus prophecy comes to leave the cult behind altogether:

Jehovah is not a God who requires sacrifice and offerings, who can be bribed by these things ... What he demands of Israel is something of universal validity, namely righteousness; what he hates is injustice and wickedness; the offence against the Godhead, sin, is entirely moral in its nature. It consists ... in a breach of the duty which man owes to man. It is morality through which alone all human society can endure. It is not a postulate, not an idea; it is at once both necessity and reality, the most vital and most personal power – Jehovah Sabaoth. Angry and destructive, the holy reality stakes its claim; it destroys both illusion and vanity (*IJG*, p. 113).

The prophets are the harbingers of an 'ethical monotheism'; they know Yahweh as the guarantor of a universally valid and universally human righteousness, and before this righteousness Israel's prerogatives fall away – or rather, they actually turn into the opposite of prerogatives: because Israel was the only people to be made conversant with this righteousness, she is called all the more strictly to account.

The prophets are the first great individualists; they raise their voices as isolated figures, requiring what they have newly recognized as being the demand of God. But the rank and file turn a deaf ear to them. The religious development of the masses, of which mention has already been made, becomes unnatural and degenerate. Deuteronomy and the movement bound up with it cuts the cult off completely from its natural roots. In the Priestly writing the cult is an end in itself, remote from life and the enemy of life. Wellhausen speaks of the hierarchy; and out of hierarchy nomocracy – the lordship of the law – developed. The devout Jew, meticulously scrupulous in his care to fulfil the law, is completely alienated from real life; his existence has its foundations in the senselessness of incomprehensible regulations.

Of course, Wellhausen sees exceptions. For example, he characterizes the attitude of the worshipper in Psalm 73 as follows:

'The life surrendered is here found again in a higher life, without any expression of hope in a hereafter. Against death and the devil, the inner certainty of union with God is cast into the scale. That is admittedly a stage of religion which is only true for a few; at least it goes far beyond the borders of Judaism' (*IJG*, p. 224).

Individuals are therefore capable of arriving at a deeper religious insight in the midst of a denaturalizing process.

In his account of Jesus, Wellhausen stresses above all the link with the ideas of the prophets; but in Jesus these are tremendously expanded. He is able to express in the simple language of the wise not only original and universal human values, but the limitless sovereignty of God.

2. Problems of Literary Criticism in the Pentateuch

The literary character of the Priestly writing (P)

(a) P as the basic narrative in the Pentateuch. Today it is largely accepted that the narrative of the Priestly writing in the Pentateuch has been preserved more or less intact. It forms the basis, the scaffolding of the Pentateuch as a whole: it has been enriched by other sources and additional material, which have disturbed the work's cohesion and destroyed its clear structure.

The reconstruction of the Priestly narrative in the book of Genesis presents no difficulties worth mentioning. P begins with a detailed account of the creation. The enumeration of a genealogy from the first man down to Noah builds the transition to a further event, which is described in ample detail: the flood. P proceeds in a similar way through the rest of Genesis: relatively detailed stories alternate with brief transitional passages, consisting of genealogies, lists and short 'linking' comments. From Exodus onwards there are uncertainties about the assignment of particular sections of the text to P. One passage, clearly deriving from P, describes the call of Moses and his charge to liberate Israel (Ex. 6.2-12; 7.1-7). The share of the Priestly document in the story of the plagues is also clear enough. But in the account of the actual exodus, evidence of language and material is too uncertain for a clear assignment to be possible, and scholarly opinion is correspondingly divided. At all events the most space is taken up by the description of the events on Sinai, which are also undoubtedly of primary importance. The enactment of the regulations for the cult, the making and consecration of cultic objects and the installation of the priests form the centre of P.

Opinions are again divided about where P ends. The death of Moses is certainly reported in brief (Deut. 34.7-9). Whether in addition large sections from Joshua 13-20 are to be counted as part of the work is disputed; it is difficult to form a judgment because there is no narrative here whose linguistic character could be compared with other narrative sections of P; there are only compilations in the form of lists.

(b) Interpolated legal material. The narrative flow of the Priestly writing is interrupted here and there. In many passages, legal material with more or less appropriate themes has been interpolated into the description. Thus, for example, it seemed the obvious course to link the description of the first sacrifice of the newly invested priests with the legal regulations about sacrifice in general (Lev. 1-7). These sacrificial instructions quite obviously interrupt the narrative. The literary explanation of fragments of this kind therefore employs the supplementary hypothesis.

(c) The intention behind P. The very name 'Priestly writing' brings out the specific interest of this narrative work: in the centre stands the cult, the office and work of the priest, who mediates between God and Israel. The considered progress of the narrative,

in which every detail has importance and in which every idea is precisely weighed up and sharply differentiated, entitles us to the supposition that here Priestly theological circles were expressing their self-understanding and their understanding of the world.

The structure of the work is strictly regular; the theme of *b^erīt* ('obligation'; the translation 'covenant' is not correct) imposes form on all events, which develop progressively upwards from the creation of the world to the people of Israel.

As we have already mentioned, Wellhausen first termed the Priestly writing Q, an abbreviation for *quattuor*, referring to the 'Book of the four covenants'. Thus he believed that he could establish the existence of four covenants. But the conclusion of a *b^erīt* through Yahweh is only mentioned explicitly twice (Gen. 9.1-17; Gen. 17). There is also talk of a *b^erīt* in connection with the giving of the law on Sinai; the obligation to keep the sabbath holy which is mentioned here no doubt stands proxy for all the cultic laws (Ex. 31.12ff.; the passage may perhaps have been interpolated into the P narrative at a secondary stage).

What, then, does the history of the world and of salvation which takes its structure from the divinely appointed *b^erīt* look like? In the creation of the world, God (who is always called *'elōhīm* in the early stages of his acts of revelation) first of all gives it an order and enforces the basic rhythm of seven days. After the rampant growth of sin and the punishment of the flood, he issues a prohibition against eating blood and binds himself never again to destroy the world; the relationship of obligation is symbolically confirmed by the rainbow (Gen. 9.8ff.). In a third stage of development God turns to Abraham; his further revelation is expressed in the communication of the divine name *'el šaddai*. God pledges himself to provide for the increase of Abraham's descendants; and the obligation is laid on Abraham to have himself and his descendants circumcised (this is at the same time the token of the new relationship). In a revelatory act of ultimate validity, God employs Moses as mediator; he gives his real name, Yahweh. Now that the true Yahweh cult has been introduced, Moses causes the cultic institutions to be set up and invests the priests.

The sequence of these stages of revelation, each surpassing the other, is brought out by a system of numbers, which exactly fixes history in time, from the creation onwards. Every person and every event has its precisely determinable place in the divine plan of salvation.

(d) The P narrative as a literary whole. The consensus of scholarly opinion about the scope and character of P is due to the fact that the conception visible in the work, and the theological intention that moulds it, is clearly expressed, not only in content but also in language. P has its particular vocabulary, and again and again makes use of the same concepts, which are consistently expressed in the same language.

It is true that there are tensions from time to time, suggesting that older sources stood behind P – sources perhaps varying in kind; but all this is none the less moulded in sovereign manner into a unified literary work. In some places we gain the impression that secondary expansions are also present; but these are stamped by the spirit of the rest of the narrative to such an extent that they are of no great importance.

It is not difficult to date P; Wellhausen's assessment has stood the test. We are dealing here with a theological outline which, during the crisis evoked by the exile and the religious and national insecurity that succeeded it, puts forward a programme of cultic restoration designed to re-establish the relationship between Israel and Yahweh.

The literary character of Deuteronomy

(a) The special place of Deuteronomy in the Pentateuch. Deuteronomy differs in external appearance from the books that precede it by claiming to be almost entirely an extensive address by Moses. At its centre is the recital of a law, framed and permeated by admonition.

From the beginning of the nineteenth century onwards, facts were discovered which made the special position of Deuteronomy in the Pentateuch clear: some of the demands made within the law are conspicuously fulfilled by the reforms of King Josiah, shortly before the exile (so the account in II Kings 22f.). In these reforms, just as in the Deuteronomic law, the confinement of the legitimate

Yahweh cult to the temple in Jerusalem plays an important part ('centralization of the cult'). The strict prohibition of worship of the heavenly bodies, the rejection of all temple prostitutes, both male and female, and the profanation of the places of child sacrifice near Jerusalem are further points which are demanded by Deuteronomy and which according to the account in the book of Kings were carried out by Josiah.

All this seemed to make it clear that Deuteronomy corresponds to the law according to which Josiah carried through his cultic reforms; according to II Kings 22.8ff., this law was found in the temple (but see p. 20 below). On the other hand, it became evident that some sections *must* have derived from the post-exilic period; chs. 29f., for example, are quite clearly a reflection of a post-exilic situation: the catastrophe threatened if the people were disobedient towards Yahweh has come to pass, and Israel is scattered among the nations. On the basis of observations of this kind, the view came to prevail that Deuteronomy is not a single literary unit.

(b) Literary stratification in Deuteronomy. An analytical observation of detail shows very quickly that even the introduction to the body of the law (chs. 1-11) is not a unity. There are actually two introductions, one beginning in 1.1 and the other in 4.44. There are stylistic differences between the two. Whereas in 1.1ff., for example, the Israelites are addressed throughout as 'you' (pl.), in 4.44ff. the singular 'thou' is generally applied to them, in a collective sense. In content, too, fine distinctions have been observed. The differentiation between 'thou' and 'you' passages comes to be an important literary criterion of distinction, and we may assume that the 'thou' passages belong to an earlier stage in the transmission. The first of the two introductions is accordingly the later, and the second, older introduction has been revised in places by the 'you' (pl.) stratum.

These problems cannot be described in detail here; they are difficult, and their solution is at many points a matter of dispute. What is important is the recognition that various strata or layers of tradition are to be found here, strata which sometimes can indeed be separated from one another quite easily, but which are very similar not only in vocabulary and thought but also in theological intention. Deuteronomy is anything but a unified literary creation; it is a documentation of a *literary development*. Later elements stand side by side with earlier ones, striving to absorb and interpret them, sometimes even trying to lead in a rather different direction. In some passages the different strata cannot be clearly divided from one another; in the older introduction and in explanatory additions to the law, the expansions of the later stratum and the earlier basic text often flow into one another without a break. We therefore have to reckon, not only with additions but also with *revision* and *recasting*.

Summing up, we can assume that originally the Deuteronomic law was furnished with an introduction (and probably also with a concluding catalogue of blessings and curses, for the observation or neglect of the provisions of the law); that an expansion and recasting then took place (above all the first introductory discourse), and that this was followed at a still later period by further expansions (for example 31.1-13).

(c) Basic theological ideas. On the whole, the main theological concerns remain the same in all strata: Yahweh alone is Israel's God, and any worship of other gods (apparently *the* temptation of the time) is resisted as fiercely as possible. Yahweh's commandments are to be strictly observed and hence emphatically enjoined by means of a stereotyped but constantly changing vocabulary. When through its behaviour Israel keeps its relationship to Yahweh in order, it arrives at the enjoyment of all the blessings which Yahweh has promised from of old: it receives and keeps the promised land, it remains successful in the struggle against its enemies, it lives in peace, prosperity and security. Disobedience, on the other hand, leads to catastrophe. The demand for centralization plays a role of differing importance in the individual strata.

(d) The writers of Deuteronomy. One must be careful not to approach the text of Deuteronomy with a modern picture of authorship in mind. We are not dealing here with authors who want to create their *own* text, distinguishable from others in quality and

intention. Older literary material is assimilated and altered as a complete matter of course; although the ruling ideas remain the same, a reworking of this kind naturally leads to subtle differences in style and content. This also provides the reason for the un-certainty in the literary-critical analysis of Deuteronomy.

The difference between the Priestly writing and Deuteronomy must be emphasized. Whereas the Priestly writing seen as a whole presents a self-contained literary outline, Deuteronomy displays a process of literary growth through a number of different strata, a process which certainly extended over decades.

(e) The dating of the Deuteronomic law.

It should be pointed out, however briefly, that the connection between the Deuteronomic law and Josiah's reform is not as clear as it seems to be at first, and as is largely assumed today. O. Kaiser has once more raised the problems that exist here, taking up points noticed by earlier scholars. Is Deuteronomy only the utterance of the Jewish community in Palestine, which was consolidating itself after the catastrophe of the exile and seeking to clarify its relationship to Yahweh? How, in this case, ought we to interpret the account in the book of Kings about Josiah's reforms? Here many questions are still open.

(f) Deuteronomy and the Deuteronomistic movement.

The main theological themes just mentioned as belonging to Deuteronomy in its various strata are not found in Deuteronomy alone. We come across them in other books as well, particularly in Joshua – II Kings. A similar vocabulary and special stylistic features belonging to them also recur. These theological and linguistic features are called *Deuteronomistic*. The Deuteronomistic share in the indivi-dual books from Joshua to II Kings varies; in the book of Judges, for example, the Deuteronomistic element appears in the transition from one 'saviour story' to another, in a stereotyped treatment of a basic Deuteronomistic idea. Israel's disobedience is followed by punishment; repentance is followed by the saving action of Yahweh, who sends a deliverer to liberate the people. In the books of Kings, in the same stereotyped fashion, every king is judged according to his faithfulness to Yahweh and his attitude towards the command for centralization. In addition, there are whole stories which exude the Deuteronomistic spirit (e.g. Josh. 11). On the other hand, long sections, e.g. in the book of Samuel, show hardly any traces of Deuteronomistic concerns.

Martin Noth has attempted to show that in the complex of books from Deuteronomy to II Kings we have a work edited by a *single* hand, the hand of the Deuteronomist. The Deuteronomist would therefore have to be conceived of as collector and editor. He first of all composes the introduction to his work (Deut. 1-4.40), then adds the Deuteronomic law, which is already furnished with an introduction and which he edits here and there. After that other material follows in the work – the narratives about the settlement in the promised land in the book of Joshua, the stories of the Judges, etc. Noth has undoubtedly drawn attention to a number of details which make it seem probable that there is continuity in the Deuteronomistic composition from Deuteronomy to II Kings; on the other hand, Deuteronomistic work on the different material varies so much that it is difficult to view this Deuteronomistic editorial treatment as a unified procedure. Here, too, the notion of successive reworkings and refashionings is more probable.

Deuteronomic language is to be found in a number of psalms, and the same may be said of many of the prophetic writings; in addition, the historical books of Chronicles may also be interpreted as a late form of the Deuteronomistic approach.

What, therefore, first manifests itself in Deuteronomy as a phenomenon of literary development, now proves to be the *written expression of an intellectual movement*, characterized by a highly unified style of thought and language, but which none the less naturally displays itself in different modes of utterance and in different forms of development. It is certainly present in the exilic and post-exilic period; but up to now there has been little clarification of its roots in pre-exilic times (cf. further pp. 137f.).

The literary character of the early sources

It is beyond question that, even if we exclude the P sections of the material in the books of Genesis, Exodus and Numbers, no unified literary narrative takes shape. The difficulties which criticism of the Pentateuch has laid bare still exist: doublets and contradictions are still only partly eradicated.

One of the main features which can be found in the course of differentiating between the various sources is the use of the divine name. One source uses the proper name of God, Yahweh, from the very beginning; the others only allow this name to become known through God's revelation to Moses, and use *'elōhīm* in the patriarchal narratives. Accordingly, scholars speak of the *Yahwist* and the *Elohist*.

But even after the material of these two sources has been separated, we are still not left with works which could be compared in unity with, say, P. This has led some scholars to make further subdivisions: there has been talk of two Yahwists, and sometimes even of two Elohists. There is some unanimity over the Elohist, so we can start there.

The Elohist

It is largely recognized today (*a*) that there is an Elohist and (*b*) that there is *only one* Elohist. Yet it is only in the book of Genesis that a few unequivocal E-complexes of some length are present. And it is here, accordingly, that the criteria for the assignment of a text to this source are to be found.

(*a*) *The characteristics of the Elohist in Genesis*. In the sections Gen. 20.1-17; 21.6,8-34; 22.1-14 *'elōhīm* is used almost exclusively as the term for God.

There are certainly some exceptions. The name Yahweh occurs in 20.18, but here we probably have a gloss (i.e. an explanation which was inserted subsequently). In 21.33 the name Yahweh occurs beside another name for God, El Olam, and thus also appears to be a superfluous gloss. A divine name other than Yahweh may possibly once have stood in 22.11, 14, where a proper name for the deity appears to be absolutely essential because of the explanation of the place-name. To sum up: the criterion of the divine name cannot be applied with complete consistency. There is a remainder which has to be explained in terms of a later revision.

Introductions give the term 'maid' or 'concubine' as one of the few further linguistic features in which J and E differ. In 21.12

this figure is called '*āmā*, whereas the Yahwist term is *šipḥā*.

But the Elohistic section in Gen. 20-22 is also marked by its unified intention. In the first place, the moral integrity of all concerned is notable. The conflicts described are not due to human failings; they spring from a divine dispensation. Abraham's lie is only a half (un)truth. The expulsion of Hagar, which could cast a slur on Abraham's character, is approved by God himself. Even Sarah, who instigates the expulsion, does not act in her own interest (say out of jealousy, as in Gen. 16 J), but spurred on by love for her son. Even subsidiary characters behave extremely honourably, and they too are protected by God's providence: Abimelech, the Canaanite city king, for example, and Hagar, with her son Ishmael.

Characteristic of the Elohist is the distance between man and God, which comes out quite clearly in comparison with other early sections of the Pentateuch. God does not encounter man directly, but in dreams. He acts from heaven, but only indirectly, through a messenger. Accordingly it is not a matter of course for a man to find access to God: Abimelech needs the intercession of Abraham, who is called a prophet (*nābī'*). In the Joseph story, too, we have a considerable narrative complex from the Elohist's pen; this becomes especially clear in Gen. 40.1-41.3. Elohistic characteristics are found in the term used for God ('*elōrīm*); in the occurrence of dreams as the medium of revelation; and in the fact that the interpretation of the dream can only be accomplished by Joseph, the mediator appointed by God.

It is noticeable how some clearly Elohistic fragments are systematically linked with one another. Thus, for example, in 31.13 the scene described in 28.10ff. is picked up again through a retrospect in the form of a reminiscent discourse.

All this points to a planned composition, which can be separated out linguistically as well as in content. But little material is as clearly Elohistic as this. Taken together, it comprises perhaps about four chapters.

Apart from these clearly Elohistic narrative sections, there are other passages in the book of Genesis which are more difficult to assign; '*elōhīm* often occurs, but other criteria speaking in favour of E are lacking. Gen. 37 might be mentioned as an example of an uncertain division of sources. Here we clearly have two stories which can be detached from one another; two reasons are given for the brothers' jealousy: on the one hand the beautiful coat which Jacob gives Joseph, and on the other Joseph's dreams (vv. 5-11). In view of the Elohist's partiality for dreams, the sources will be assigned accordingly. But any more definite criteria are lacking.

(b) The Elohist sections in Exodus and Numbers. Here the separating out of E material by the methods of literary criticism is comparably more difficult than in Genesis. This is first because the criterion of the divine name can no longer be reliably applied: in Ex. 3 (scholars are agreed in assigning vv. 4b, 6, 9-14 to E) God reveals himself with his name, Yahweh. But there continue to be further passages which are conspicuous in using only *'elōhīm*.

See e.g. Ex. 13. 17-19. In the Sinai story (Ex. 19; 20. 18ff.; 24) one narrative thread seems to be characterized by the use of *'elōhīm*. The messenger of God (*mal'āk̲ 'elōhīm*) familiar from Genesis turns up again in 14.19a. In the Balaam story, too (Num. 22f.), the Elohistic sections can be separated out on the basis of the divine name (though admittedly in some passages we have to start from textual variants which presuppose *'elōhīm* in place of the proper name).

In addition, however, we now find passages in which *Yahweh* and *'elōhīm* occur in parallel to one another, and it is impossible to distinguish the sources from one another.

See e.g. Ex. Only *'elōhīm* is used in the main section of this story (vv. 13-27). But the position is different in vv. 1-12; here both terms are found side by side. In addition, there are unevennesses in the fabric of the text. In spite of this it is impossible to separate out the text as we now have it into two independent and meaningful sources.

Certain sections are often assigned to E without any use of the criterion of the divine name. Thus, for example, parts of the story of the plagues and the account of the passage through the Reed Sea are held by certain scholars to be Elohistic, and the same can be said of sections within Num. 11f., which associate Moses with prophetic phenomena. In all these passages Yahweh is used throughout for the name of God (Ex. 14.19a is an exception). E is therefore arrived at either for reasons connected with the content (Num. 11f.: closeness to prophecy, which might possibly be supported by Gen. 20.7), or by eliminating other possible attributions. At all events, it it obvious that the Elohist's work is far less clearly in evidence in Exodus and Numbers than in Genesis (see further pp. 29f. below).

Yahwist and Yahwists

(a) Tensions in content. When we have separated out the Priestly writing and the Elohist sections, material remains which is continually marked by stresses and strains.

For example, the story of the 'peril of the mother of the race' is to be found twice, in Gen. 12.10ff. and 26.6-11. Within the story of the garden of Eden and the fall, God's cursing of man is clearly described in two different ways.

For this reason, attempts have been made to divide up the Yahwistic stratum further. According to this view, we should reckon with two Yahwistic writings. The terminology is not unified. R. Smend (the author of this so-called 'latest documentary hypothesis') talked about J^1 and J^2; O. Eissfeldt called the source J^1 'the lay source' (abbreviation L); G. Fohrer sees it as a 'nomadic source stratum' (abbreviation N). The symbol J is generally used for J^2.

Of course the symbols L or N designate one characteristic of this source – *the* typical characteristic, which differentiates it from other Yahwistic material. This characteristic relates to the content; linguistic criteria for the differentiation which could be established between J and E, even if they were few in number, are almost totally lacking and are uncertain. For this reason one is on somewhat shaky ground with these hypotheses.

(b) Tensions in the cultural ideal. Some texts clearly reflect the nomadic way of life, or even a nomadic ideal of life.

For example, in the supplementary passage about the expulsion from the garden of Eden, the curse which lies over human destiny (in the one version) is clearly seen from the nomadic point of view (Gen. 3. 18-19aα). Chapter 4.17-24 is the expression of nomadic cultural achievements and the desert dweller's unfettered thirst for revenge (which is understood in a positive sense). According to 9.21-27 the outstanding product of the cultivated soil, wine, immediately leads to corruption: it produces incestuous homosexuality, the very quintessence of all moral degeneracy. The deed is followed by its curse.

In contrast, there are sections in which the life of the settled arable farmer is at the centre of the picture.

For example, in the story about the expulsion from the Garden of Eden mentioned above, human misery is also described from the point of view of the tiller of the ground (Gen. 3.17, 19aβ,b). The story of Cain and Abel clearly shows more sympathy for Abel, the farmer, than for his dangerous brother, whose life is interpreted as a curse (Gen. 4.1-16).

There is therefore a series of stories which presuppose or idealize either one or the other way of life. Here tension is undoubtedly present. On the other hand, of course, in most of the stories the underlying cultural view is not brought out at all explicitly. So other aspects of the tensions within the Yahwistic material must be brought to bear.

(c) Tensions in the degree of reflection. If we attempt to outline the understanding of God in the Yahwistic stratum, we also arrive at a discordant picture. In the story of creation Yahweh is depicted anthropomorphically. He goes for a walk in the cool of the evening, looks for man, fails to find him, so calls him; and so forth. On the other hand, in the Yahwist's account of the passage through the Red Sea, Yahweh does not act at all in the direct sense (in contrast to the Song of Miriam, for example, Ex. 15.21). He forces back the sea's water by means of an east wind; the divine action is mediated through natural events – marvellous ones, no doubt, but quite within the bounds of normal experience (Ex. 14.21 aβ).

Thus in this respect, too, it is possible to seek criteria for a division of the sources. One starting point is the assumption that the source N is marked by the 'incorporation of archaic narrative material with nomadic traits' (Fohrer, *Introduction to the Old Testament*, p. 162). 'The God of the desert, who can be worshipped truly only in the milieu of the nomadic way of life, exhibits strikingly anthropomorphic traits. In the primal history especially

Yahweh is concerned for his power; for this reason he banishes man from the Garden of God and scatters mankind throughout the earth. The narratives of Jacob's wrestling and the ambush on Moses, which have been applied to Yahweh, could also occur in no other source stratum' (ibid, p. 164; cf. here Gen. 11.1-9; 32,24b-32; Ex. 4.24-26).

Primitively simple thinking therefore turns into an additional criterion for the separation of the sources; it belongs to the nomadic cultural ideal. But often enough it becomes evident that an evaluation of the texts in this respect is largely subject to aesthetic sensibility and is not easy to check.

One example may serve to indicate the difficulties which arise in the application of this criterion for distinguishing between the sources. Anyone who reckons with two J sources will try to dissect Gen. 18f. into two different strands. There are quite enough tensions in the content to justify the attempt. In the one version, two (or three) men (manifestations of Yahweh? Messengers from Yahweh?) encounter Abraham; in the other, Yahweh is explicitly named as Abraham's partner in the discussion. We encounter an anthropomorphic picture of God in *both* versions; any spiritualization of the idea of God (such as is present in Ex. 14.21aβ, for instance) is completely lacking.

(d) One Yahwist or two? The manifold tensions within the Yahwist's work make it clear that in any event we cannot assume that we are dealing with a self-contained literary draft, comparable with the Priestly writing. The division into two sources is one solution of the problem. It has its weaknesses: the criteria for distinguishing between the sources are highly general in kind; they cannot be applied to all the texts and to a high degree are at the mercy of subjective feeling.

The single-Yahwist hypothesis has to explain the manifold tensions in a different way: we must then assume that the Yahwist has hardly touched the material that has come down to him (sagas, folk-tales, etc.) in the course of committing it to writing. In that case it would be quite conceivable that the variety of material used by J should be characterized by very varying characteristics and purposes, which give rise to a somewhat discordant total impression. Similarly, tensions within a story (for example Gen. 18f.) would not have to be explained by the methods of literary criticism; they would come under the history of the tradition (cf. pp. 51ff.).

In that case, we should have to look for the specific Yahwistic characteristics and purpose in the writer's ordering of his material and in the bridge passages. Thus the content of the primaeval history, for example, shows a clear trend: it displays a constant series of human rebellions against God and punitive, yet continually merciful, reactions on the part of Yahweh. The nadir of events (the building of the tower of Babel) is followed by the story of the promises to the patriarchs, which we meet in continually new variations from Gen. 12 onwards. Here, therefore, are manifested yet again the gracious acts of Yahweh, which are to reach beyond Israel to the whole world of the nations.

This conception admittedly implies a Yahwist whose characteristics are as complex as it is possible to conceive. We must assume on the one hand that he forms his work in subjection to a sovereign, over-riding plan; that he allows his considered understanding of God to shine through here and there – and on the other hand that he absorbs archaic tales unaltered into his design. At all events, we can by no means arrive at a self-contained picture comparable with say the picture of the Elohist which emerges from Gen. 20ff.

Placing the early Pentateuchal sources

We can only cast a brief glance at the question of the date and place of origin of the early sources of the Pentateuch. Most scholars have arrived at an astonishing consensus of opinion here. J is usually put in the period of David and Solomon; its place of origin is thought to be the territory of the tribe of Judah. If one reckons with two Yahwistic sources, the picture becomes more complicated; Eissfeldt sees L as the earliest source (tenth-ninth century) and J as somewhat later. Fohrer, on the other hand, considers J the earlier (850-800) and views N as being the slightly later conservative reaction. E is generally assigned to the northern kingdom, its closeness to early prophecy being stressed.

All attempts at dating the sources have to work with relatively weak arguments. Direct pointers to contemporary conditions are almost completely lacking (for J, Gen. 15.18 and Num. 24.17f. are often cited; but these are not particularly conclusive). For this reason scholars generally have to make use of *argumenta e silentio* for the date (i.e., have to argue from what is *not* to be found in the material), and must also draw on general considerations based on the history of ideas. It is possible to point to the evolution of the prophetic idea in the northern kingdom and, in E on the one hand and J on the other, to the rationality of the idea of God in the 'period of the Enlightenment under David and Solomon'. Definite clues pointing to a certain date are therefore lacking. The attempt at a methodologically thought-out classification of material in relationship to other Old Testament literature is a task for the future.

J and E – some conclusions

Deuteronomy and the Priestly writing are examples of two completely different literary types: on the one hand we have the work of a *single* author (or at least of an entirely homogeneous group of writers), on the other the documentation of a literary development. How are J and E to be classified?

In places E seems to be as much of an entity as P. At other points, however, this characteristic is no longer evident. In J the situation is still more difficult. Whether one now reckons with one or two J sources, the cohesion and systematic intention is not readily recognizable. Recently a suspicion has been expressed that J was already working with written sources (for indications see Kaiser, § 8.4).

One observation must be added. Both Elohistic and Yahwistic material show signs of additions here and there which are clearly recognizable as being the addenda of a later period (for example Gen. 22.15-19, as an addition to E; Ex. 13.1-16, as an addition to J). Moreover, we must also remember passages like Ex. 18 where, although we do not have a smooth, straightforward text, the problems cannot be satisfactorily solved by a separation of the sources; here we should rather assume a revision by a later hand.

Generally speaking, we may perhaps draw the conclusion that in the early source writings we must not assume that what we have are undamaged component parts of the original source. Revisions and recastings may sometimes also be present, very similar to what we found in Deuteronomy. At all events, the history of the ancient source writings seems to have taken a more complicated course than the classical solutions are capable of indicating. The 'redactors', or editors, have not only put the material together, making unimportant additions here and there; they have sometimes apparently intervened in the transmission of the text through a more considerable moulding of the material.

In addition we must take into account the fact that the findings of literary criticism with regard to the ancient sources are anything but homogeneous throughout. We have pointed out that in Gen. 20ff. a relatively clear E complex is present. It is possible to see a J complex (though a disputed one) in the primaeval history. In the Joseph story the mixture of the two sources E and J is relatively clear. But it is certainly a mistake to approach every text with the presupposition that it must be compiled from several sources, or that it must fit the trend of one of the hypothetical sources. The attribution of a text to a source is the final exegetical step, not the first one. And in this attribution it should be possible to name several criteria (linguistic and stylistic features; ideas typical of the source; links with the context). The greater the number of criteria in a given text which can be produced in favour of inclusion in a certain source, the more probable the literary judgment becomes.

One problem has become evident at various points in our discussion of the problems surrounding the early sources of the Pentateuch. In what way have these writers absorbed already fashioned material into their work? What kind of material was it? How did it reach the writers? And what was their aim in writing at all? These questions go beyond the problems of literary criticism (see pp. 36ff. below).

3. Literary Criticism in the Prophetic Books

The starting point

In the prophetic writings the literary-critical questions developed somewhat differently from those of the Pentateuch. Here one was dealing with authors who were known by name; as a rule the prophetic writings at least state when their writer lived and where he came from. Sometimes one or the other episode from the prophet's life is related, and in this way his words and acts are known. Here it seemed the obvious course to enquire into the connections between a prophet's words and his effects on his time. In this way the whole prophetic personality was to be made available to modern understanding. This concern more or less characterizes the original literary-critical approach to the prophetic writings.

Here is a first *example* from the history of research. A study which appeared in 1712 proved that Jeremiah could not possibly be the author of Lamentations. Up to that point this had been assumed as a matter of course. (It is true that Jeremiah is never expressly named as author in the text itself, but *threnoi Ieremiou* appears in the Septuagint tradition either as title or signature, depending on the individual manuscripts.) The argument runs as follows. The book contains laments that there is no longer any prophetic revelation; but this is what Jeremiah claims for himself. Lamentations expresses horror that Jerusalem has been quite unexpectedly captured by the enemy; but Jeremiah had always reckoned with this catastrophe – and so on. The picture of Jeremiah which can be drawn from the sayings and narratives of the book of Jeremiah does not fit into the thought-world of Lamentations. Consequently Jeremiah can be eliminated as author. In a similar way, people also learnt to distinguish between Isaiah and Deutero-Isaiah (Isa. 40-55), etc.

'Authenticity'

The central concept in the literary criticism of the prophetic writings is 'authenticity'. Everything that goes back to the prophet himself counts as being 'authentic'; later additions are 'inauthentic'. Moreover, a value judgment is bound up with the distinction between authenticity and inauthenticity, especially in the exegetical literature of the nineteenth and early twentieth century (and even today a judgment of this kind can still be detected). The 'authentic' passages are alone taken to be of value; only they correspond to the personality of the prophet in whom the exegete is interested. The inauthentic parts, on the other hand, obscure insight into the prophetic character and are a later falsification of the utterances of the original.

Behind value judgments of this kind there is, of course, a

quite particular picture of the prophet. The prophet is viewed as a 'religious genius'; it is the task of exegetical work to bring out what is unmistakably unique about him. Here the 'inauthentic' sections are bound to seem troublesome; they have importance for the exegetical process only in so far as they have to be excluded (for a qualification of this point of view which is to some extent justifiable, see pp. 34f.).

The scholar moves in a circle over the question of the criteria of authenticity. First of all he needs a basic stock of texts whose genuineness he can assume (e.g. he excludes all material which relates to historical situations which the prophet cannot have experienced; he excludes material in which ideas and concepts occur which the prophet cannot yet have known, and so on). In particular, he has to collect texts which in some way or other differ as a whole from other groups of Old Testament texts (though common features of style or type of argument). Here, therefore, something like a profile of the personality of the prophet as writer – a profile recorded in the text – is built up. By means of this profile other texts, whose authenticity is more questionable, will now be judged.

Amos

The book of Amos may serve as an example. Throughout, it is determined by almost continuous threats of disaster to Israel. The prophet bases these primarily on Israel's wrong conduct. The ordinances of the law are not observed, the mighty commit acts of violence against the weak, the rich lead their extravagantly luxurious lives at the cost of the poor. In the face of this situation, Yahweh's will towards destruction is inescapable, and Israel's allegedly special position is rescinded. Destruction is inevitable. Here Amos apparently addresses only to the inhabitants of the northern kingdom, although he himself came from the southern kingdom.

That is an outline of the basic tenor of Amos' message. Now a few passages, which do not speak so unconditionally about disaster, stand out quite clearly. They suggest the possibility that Yahweh might perhaps after all exercise mercy: 'Seek good, and not evil, that you may live; and so Yahweh, the God of hosts, will be with you, as you have said. Hate evil, and love good, and establish justice in the gate; it may be that Yahweh, the God of hosts, will be gracious to the remnant of Joseph' (Amos 5.14f., cf. already vv. 4-6). Here, then, there is no unconditional prediction of disaster; there is a last call to repentance, a possibility of salvation is presented to the hearer in the form of a 'perhaps'. Here is Hans Walter Wolff's comment: 'A prophetic disciple belonging to the wisdom school might talk in this reserved, almost sceptical way – but not a prophet of the stamp of Amos' (*Dodekapropheton* 2, 1969, p. 295). Verse 13 then fits the well-weighed caution of this prophetic disciple quite well: 'Therefore he who is prudent will keep silent in such a time; for it is an evil time.' The discreet sage prefers to hold his peace when he gets into difficulties. How can this be reconciled with Amos, the uncompromising proclaimer of Yahweh's truth?

The close of the book of Amos (9.8-15) even talks definitely about salvation. The literary critics are correspondingly sceptical. Well-hausen's judgment has become a classic:

'Roses and lavender instead of blood and iron ... I do not believe that 9.8-15 derives from Amos. After 9.1-4,7 he cannot suddenly say, it was not meant to be taken so seriously, everything will turn out splendidly after all; for he is not joking in those verses. He is speaking with deadly seriousness; he means what he says. After he has just gone far beyond all his earlier threats, he cannot suddenly blunt their impact, he cannot let milk and honey flow from the cup of Yahweh's wrath. He is unique in looking doom in the face and he understands that for him the downfall of Israel means the victory of Yahweh – and now, after the boldest flight of this faith of his, is he to sink back tamely into the very delusion that he is fighting? Is now the illusion to triumph over its destroyer, the God of what men would like to be true, over the God of historical necessity? It was rather a later Jew who attached the coda, supplanting the real end, because it rang too harshly in his ears' (*Die Kleinen Propheten*, 1898, p. 96).

But now the reverse argument has been used for this very passage. The theory runs roughly as follows: when Amos talks at all, he does so with a particular purpose and this purpose can only be motivated by the desire to make Israel come to its senses for the last time. According to this argument the possibility of salvation would be constitutive for the prophet's message. Even 5.13 can be defended: Amos is actually talking to himself here. He knows that a sensible man would now hold his tongue, because it is too late to speak. But as a prophet, Amos *has* to speak, at Yahweh's command. Even the closing passage is held to be genuine by some scholars; these point out that Amos' place of origin was Judah: he announces the downfall of the northern kingdom, but reckons with the salvation and restoration of the united Davidic empire.

There are therefore often differences in sketching the outline of a prophet's personality, and judgment about the authenticity of particular passages will accordingly be a matter of dispute. In a discussion about authenticity, importance must always be attached on the fact that what is in question is bound to be the outline of *writers'* personalities; exactly the same attention must therefore be paid to linguistic usage, style, etc., as to content. Cf. the analogous problems in the Pentateuch (pp. 25f. above).

In the book of Amos especially there are instructive examples of the way in which inauthenticity can be proved through the simultaneous observation of content and the way it is expressed. Closer observation shows that a Deuteronomistic stratum of revision is present in a series of passages. Here ideas appear which do not otherwise occur in Amos, but which are current coin in the Deuteronomistic writings; and they are formulated in language which Amos does not otherwise use but which has become conventionalized phraseology in the Deuteronomistic writings.

The literary transmission of the prophetic sayings

In their present form, the prophetic books do not go back to the prophets themselves. The process of collecting and composing the prophetic sayings seems to have extended over a considerable period. A number of hints thrown out by various prophets imply that groups of pupils formed round the different prophets; it is here that writing and the work of composition will primarily have taken place.

As we have already mentioned, in the early period literary critics hardly devoted any attention to this process. Where subject matter was added to the genuine sayings in the course of editing it was greeted as 'falsification', 'corruption', 'watering down' – in short, as 'inauthentic'.

We have meanwhile learnt to see the positive side of this process of transmission and editing. For in these later interpolations there is a clear intention to give expression to the prophetic message in a new historical situation. These inauthentic sayings therefore have an interpretative character; they take account of the fact that listeners, circumstances, historical and theological situation have altered; and they try none the less to preserve the intention of the prophetic message (cf. pp. 56f.).

This becomes clearest when we consider the people to whom the prophetic sayings of Amos and the book of Hosea were addressed. Both are directed towards the northern kingdom. In both books we find later applications of the prophetic message to the southern kingdom (at a period when the northern kingdom was no longer in existence and the prophetic sayings were being passed on in the south). For example Amos 2.4f.; Hos. 12.1, 3 (though both text and interpretation of v. 1b are in dispute!).

The prophetic books therefore contain both original prophetic words and narratives (i.e. 'authentic' passages) and their earliest interpretation within the Old Testament itself, intended for later situations. In some prophetic books this interpretative process is relatively easy to follow (e.g. Amos); in others it is exceedingly complicated, because the original sayings have not only been supplemented but also remodelled to a high degree by later interpretation (e.g. Jeremiah). The parallelism to the problems of the Pentateuch is clear.

II

Old Testament Literature
and the Community

1. *The Background*

Empirically based fields of study

The second half of the nineteenth century is marked by the first
flowering of a number of empirically based fields of study which
took on considerable importance for exegetical theology.

(a) Sociology. Sociology must be named first of all. Its theme is
the significance of the community, its institutions and norms, for
the individual. It takes account of the fact that to be understood
aright the individual cannot be taken in isolation. The mutual
interaction of individual and community must always be considered.

An impressive example of the new way of looking at things is the
work of E. Durkheim (one of the founders of modern sociology) on
suicide (1897). Here Durkheim shows statistically how social factors
(links with the community, family circumstances, stability of political
conditions, etc.) correlate in this extreme example of human behaviour.
For theology, which up to then had concentrated on the behaviour of
the individual, this kind of thinking was bound to give an important
impetus towards fresh deliberations.

(b) Psychology. During this period psychology emancipated itself
completely from philosophy. The stage of speculative psychological
work was now followed by an empirical, experimental concern with
mental and emotional processes. The aim was to discover the
elements of what goes on in the mind by means of exact observation
and self-observation.

(c) The science of religion. The science of religion also achieved its first flowering in the second half of the nineteenth century. On the one hand it tried to describe the variety of religions objectively (that is to say, independently of a judgment based on Christian values); on the other hand the aim was to discover the laws governing the structure, or even the development, of religion by means of a comparison of different religions.

The ethnologist E. B. Tylor (1832-1917) exerted an important influence on this field of studies. He postulated a general *law of religious development*; he saw its origin in animism, the belief that the whole of nature is permeated by personal or spiritual powers; a spiritual force of this kind is effective in man too (it can detach itself from the body, as is clearly evident in dreams, for example, or in death). It is essential for man to be able to deal with these forces, and to do this is the primal stage of religion. Religion has gone on developing: spirits have become gods, etc. To every cultural development corresponds a new, higher stage of religion. With this Tylor outlined an evolutionary pattern of religion corresponding to Darwin's theory of evolution in the field of biology.

Since Tylor, the pattern of religious evolution has been frequently discussed and also modified. Scholars pointed above all to a widespread conception in many religions: the idea of efficacious powers which do not possess a personal being and will. Many wanted to see these phenomena (the name frequently used is 'dynamism') as a preliminary stage to animism. In this way the theory of religious evolution would be modified but maintained in principle.

The phenomenology of religion developed in clear contrast to these often forced attempts to reconstruct religious development. Its founder was P. Chantepie de la Saussaye (1848-1920). Phenomenology seeks to observe religious phenomena irrespective of any theoretical premise; the only presupposition involved is that all religious phenomena are basically accessible to the understanding and are thereby open to interpretation in words. Through comparative description and interpretation (that is to say, through the explanation of particular manifestations) an inventory emerges of the possible ways of describing religious phenomena. Common expressions (e.g. 'magic', 'priest', 'myth') take on a sharply defined semantic character through the enquiry into their content of experience and meaning. Phenomenology therefore works out, so to speak, a grammar for the science of religion; it describes structures which make possible an understanding of religious processes and from which processes in the history of religions can then be interpreted.

The close connection between sociology, psychology, ethnology and the science of religion was felt very strongly towards the end of the nineteenth century. It is significant that pioneers of sociology and psychology offered important contributions to research into the history of religion (E. Durkheim in his book, *Les formes élémentaires de la vie religieuse*, 1906; W. Wundt in his *Völkerpsychologie*, 1900 on). But scholars concerned with phenomenology of religion were also clear that in describing the content of the experience that belongs to a religious phenomenon they could get along without psychology.

(d) Influence on theology. Here and there, the exegetical theologians of the end of the nineteenth and the beginning of the twentieth century point to results in the disciples we have mentioned; but an explicit, programmatic discussion is lacking. These disciples were chiefly influential in shaping the questions asked in Old Testament exegesis. In what way does the community affect the genesis of the Old Testament texts? What mental and emotional happenings are reflected in these texts? How are the testimonies of the religion of the Old Testament to be evaluated in the framework of a general view of religion?

Ancient oriental archaeology

The nineteenth century was the great period of discovery of the vanished civilizations of the ancient East. Excavations in Mesopotamia and Egypt were followed by the deciphering of cuneiform script and hieroglyphics. Civilizations of which men had had only a faint impression, on the basis of what had been passed down by the Old Testament and by Greek and Latin tradition, now suddenly appeared to the historian in all their clarity.

Literary discoveries, above all, were calculated to excite the interest of Old Testament scholars: a Babylonian creation story was found which in many respects resembled the Priestly account.

One tablet of the Gilgamesh epic contains a story about a great flood. Certain regulations in the code of Hammurabi are reminiscent of Old Testament edicts. All this and more was naturally a challenge to compare, and then to interpret the connections.

The history of religions school

One group of theologians took on essential importance for the progress of research into the Old Testament and for theological developments in general; the concern of this group was to see the Christian religion, from its beginnings in the faith of the Old and New Testaments, in its historical development and relativity and to draw the appropriate systematic conclusions. The movement which grew up round this purpose is known to the history of theology as the history of religions school.

In reading the Old and New Testaments, all normative historical factors were to be taken into account. Of course, it seemed obvious to include in the investigation the whole cultural environment of the times, which had been illuminated by the new archaeological discoveries. Through a comparison with this environment, it would undoubtedly be possible to work out the features peculiar to Israel with special clarity. It is therefore not the case that the discoveries in Egypt and Assyria would have led to the history of religions school; both phenomena are to be seen in the wider framework of the general intellectual history of the last century.

By setting the historical conditioning of biblical religion and the Christian faith in general in the centre of its observations, the history of religions school required a systematic clarification of the historian's task. This clarification was offered by *Ernst Troeltsch* (1865-1923). Troeltsch established the following essential principles which have to be observed in historical research. First, the principle of *criticism*. The probability of every historical fact in a tradition must be investigated. This critical investigation of sources is dependent on a comparison with happenings which come about under corresponding conditions. For no historical event is unique; analogous constellations lead to analogous events. In his observation of facts the historian has therefore to apply the *principle of analogy*. In this way he makes sure that causes and effects are rightly perceived in historical processes; the facts are linked up with one another and presented in their mutual relativity. With this the principle of *correlation* becomes effective.

These fundamental historical observations raise the question of the special character of Christianity, of the qualitative distinction between Christianity and other religions or – in the terminology of the discussion carried on at the turn of the century – of the absoluteness of Christianity. How can one judge the relation between the exclusive claim to truth of the Christian faith and the relativity of all historical happenings?

At any rate, the special position of Christianity cannot be proved in absolute and timeless terms. With the means at his command the historian may indeed be able to prove the special character of Christianity compared with other religions; he will also evaluate these special features from the angle of his own specific cultural standpoint; but again his judgment is subject to the relativity of this very standpoint. Above all, he is unable to say anything about future developments.

The ideas which have been roughly indicated here form the background of all the endeavours of the history of religions school. They were abruptly pushed aside after the First World War by the invasion of dialectical theology – and even today form part of the undigested heritage of the most recent past in the history of theology.

Hermann Gunkel

At this period the chief impulses in the sphere of Old Testament research came from Hermann Gunkel (1862-1932). He took up the whole range of ideas that stimulated his time and achieved a work which has remained of pioneer importance for Old Testament scholarship down to the present day. We shall demonstrate the new exegetical approach at three points.

(a) The History of Material: Creation. Gunkel's first important work bears the title *Schöpfung und Chaos in Urzeit und Endzeit* (Creation and chaos in the primal period and in the end-time) (1895). In the first instance Gunkel investigates the subject-matter of the

creation story in the Priestly writing. Whereas e.g. Wellhausen had regarded this as P's own invention, Gunkel now systematically followed up the connections between the creation story in P and the Babylonian creation myth *enuma elisha* (named from the opening words), which had become known a good thirty years earlier. It is true that even before Gunkel, scholars were largely unanimous in holding that there must have been connections between *enuma elisha* and Gen. 1, but literary criticism, with its particular way of thinking, had been unable to explain these connections in a plausible way.

The content of enuma elish. The myth (for a definition of myth see p. 54) first describes the chaotic primal condition of the universe. The primal deity Tiamat (=Hebrew *tehōm*) embodies the primordial waters. From the marriage with her consort Apsu, a series of generations of gods arises. Finally Marduk, the city god of Babylon, is born. Conflict arises between Tiamat and the younger gods, and Tiamat sends dragons and similar monsters – the offspring of chaos – into the struggle; finally she herself goes over to the attack. At the moment when the situation becomes critical, the gods choose Marduk for their king. He defeats Tiamat, cuts her in two (that is to say, he creates an empty space in the primordial waters) and forms the earth in the intervening space; he establishes the heavenly order, creates man (in conjunction with Ea, the god of wisdom) and builds his sanctuary, and with it the city of Babylon. The myth ends with the gods' acclamation of Marduk their king.

Gunkel established that a number of Old Testament passages talk about a struggle between God and a mythical enemy very like that in the Babylonian myth (e.g. Ps. 89.9f.; Job 26.12f.; etc.). It is true that Gen. 1 lacks anything of the kind; but in spite of that the relationship to *enuma elish* is clear. In both places the sea is the chaotic archetypal element and the picture of the world agrees, down to details into which we cannot go here.

From these observations Gunkel concludes that the Babylonian creation myth and the Priestly creation account basically reflect the same myth, but in two completely different editorial versions ('recensions'). Possible missing links may perhaps be older Israelite recensions which are to be found in the various Old Testament allusions outside P. Like the Babylonian version, these have poetic form; but it is characteristic of them that the mythological ideas have receded somewhat. Thus, for example, the idea that the power of chaos is older than Yahweh is missing in Israel. We notice a decisive break between these older versions, and P's rendering: 'Sober prose in place of archaic poetry, but at the same time a higher view of God in place of archaic naïvety' (p. 120).

It was clear to Gunkel that because of the climatic presuppositions behind the imagery, the origin of the myth was to be found in Babylon. How, then, did the myth travel, and how did the different versions come into existence? We have to consider *oral tradition*. The written testimony which we have consists only of extracts – so to speak frames from the sequence of oral tradition. Thus the differences between the various versions can easily be explained.

In the second part of his exposition Gunkel arrives at a discussion of the New Testament: he deals with Rev. 12, pointing out that here too the material of the creation myth is present, in respect of a coming perfection in the end-time which already has its roots in the Old Testament prophets. That is to say: even Gen. 1 is not the final link in the transmission of this material; the development went further, ripening into completely new variants.

In this way Gunkel traces the history of the creation myth from its Babylonian roots down to its Israelite forms. It is only then that Israel's typical religious achievement emerges – for example, the development of the image of God from an archaic materialism into the finest spiritualization, finding its expression in God's sovereign superiority over the original element, which is degraded to the mere material for creation. The comparison offered by the history of religion helps us to grasp Israel's unique character.

It is also important to notice that Gunkel already reckons with oral tradition even here, though it was only in his next major work that he followed up the precise conditions of such tradition.

(*b*) *The history of form* (*form criticism*): *the patriarchal sagas.* In 1901 Gunkel's second main work appeared: his commentary on Genesis. Gunkel takes up the results of literary-critical research, but modifies them in a characteristic way. In his view, the committal of the sagas to writing was not the unique, individual achievement of a single person; it was the work of a longer literary development. Yahwist and Elohist are not 'individuals' but 'schools' – i.e., groups of people characterized by a certain unity of thought and imagination.

This interpretation of the literary character of the sources bears fruit above all in connection with the source J. Gunkel distinguishes between the original stratum J and a later supplementary stratum, which is demonstrated e.g. by discrepancies in the geographical data. This was not Gunkel's main concern, generally speaking, and his results here have, quite unjustly, received little attention.

Gunkel is primarily concerned with the history of the Genesis material *before* it was committed to writing. While in *Schöpfung und Chaos* the form taken by oral tradition was given only marginal attention, now this aspect too moves into the centre of Gunkel's observations. Form and content are now recognized as being an inseparable whole: the passing on (and development) of the material takes particular forms; but these forms too undergo development. The attempt to view the development of the material in content and form together is indicated by the term *literary history*.

The form which we chiefly meet in Genesis is the *saga*. Briefly, Gunkel's thesis is that Genesis is a collection of sagas. We find some compressed statements about the nature of the sagas in a later shortened version of the Genesis commentary (*Die Schriften des Alten Testaments*, I/1):

The saga talks about the things which a people has at heart, about what is personal and private, and it loves to conceive political circumstances and personalities in such a way that popular interest can identify itself with them (p. 14).

We cannot and should not expect historically correct accounts; it is not the intention of saga to write history or to describe past facts reliably. Nor is its tone appropriate to sober historical writing.

For the main thing is and remains the poetical tone of these narratives. Historical writing which sets out to teach men what has really happened is in its very nature prose; but saga is in its very nature poetry: it wants to delight, to elevate, to inspire, to touch the heart. Thus those who desire to do justice to these ancient narratives must have sufficient aesthetic feeling from a story what it is and what it sets out to be (p. 16).

The form, content and intention of the Old Testament sagas are therefore to be described with the help of aesthetic sensitivity. Anyone who really wants to understand the saga must be able to enter wholly into the situation in which it was once related. Here Gunkel establishes an indissoluble connection between the situation, the intention and the form of the story. He arrives at the following terminology. He calls 'the typical narrative situation' its *Sitz im Leben* – that is, its setting in life. The linguistic form, which remains constant as long as intention and situation are also constant, is called the *Gattung*, or *genre*. Thus Gunkel arrives at the following brief characterizations. We should postulate genres, where we can establish the presence of:

1. A particular stock of ideas and moods; 2. a distinct linguistic form in which these are expressed; and 3. a setting in life which provides the essential presupposition for an understanding of content and form (*Die israelitische Literatur*, ²1925, postscript).

The establishment of the setting in life implies that we can answer the following questions:

Who is speaking? What is the audience? What mood dominates the situation? What effect is being aimed at? (*Reden und Aufsätze*, 1913, p. 33).

Quite clearly, Gunkel's questions have their sociological and psychological side. The parts played by those involved in the scene are determined; the function of a linguistic process in its particular group is analysed; the psychological processes involved are described. All these factors ultimately serve to make it possible for a person living in modern times to arrive at a systematic understanding of what is said in the past.

Gunkel later applied precisely the same questions to the psalms. Again he asks about the setting in life which is behind the individual psalms and about their living application in the ancient Israelite cult; in this way he arrives at the description of different genres among them. His chief publications here are: *Ausgewählte Psalmen*, 1904; *Die Psalmen*, HAT, 1926; *Einleitung in die Psalmen*, 1927/33 (completed by J. Begrich).

(c) The history of religion: prophecy. Gunkel expressed his views on prophecy chiefly in the introductions which he wrote for H. Schmidt's commentary *Die grossen Propheten* (SAT II/2, ²1923). In this connection we have to consider the way in which Gunkel presents prophecy as a phenomenon belonging to the history of religion in general.

Gunkel describes *ecstasy* as being the fundamental prophetic experience. The curious accompanying phenomena which the Old Testament describes in connection with the ministry of the prophets (visions, symbolic actions, abnormal movements, etc.) are the marks of ecstasy not only in Israel but throughout the world. Ecstasy can be understood:

The science of psychology is not confronted with religious ecstasy as with an incomprehensible secret; it knows that in the world there have been many religious ecstatics apart from the prophets and that every human emotion is capable of intensification to the point of ecstasy (p. XXIII).

The religious interpretation of the phenomenon of ecstasy is just as wide as ecstasy itself. It is a quite basic religious experience, even for man today when he is moved by God in a particular way. Referring to Tylor, Gunkel writes:

The scholar is not at all surprised by this, for he knows that wherever such phenomena are found in the world, they are judged to derive from the Godhead; and how should man in ancient times think differently? For anybody who is subject to such states knows well enough that here he is penetrated by something alien, something higher that lays him under some compulsion (pp. XXIVf.).

The individual prophet is distinguished from the average ecstatic of the early Israelite period.

But out of this group of prophets, individual men of nobler type arose, men capable of higher flights of thought and a greater breadth of vision. These heroes speak of the destinies of people and kings ... they are concerned with the greatest questions of which Israel was then aware. And they arrived at these questions of their own accord. The ecstatics accepted enquiries as an organized group; these mighty men among the prophets come forward independently. Hence too the exaltation with which they are imbued. Conscious as they are of being servants of God, they do not draw back (p. XXIX).

So here again a characteristic historical development is displayed: the group phenomenon of early prophecy can be compared with every random ecstatic movement on earth; but out of this developed the unmistakably Israelite phenomenon of the individual prophet in his unique grandeur. At the same time, we must not overlook the fact that in these figures too the ecstatic aspect is present.

To the degree that the prophets put their hidden experience into words, they naturally enter the sphere of Israel's literary history. Their speech is then once more stamped by its situation, its hearers, the intention behind its statements, etc. Gunkel therefore assumes that there is a certain distance between the ecstatic experience and its expression in language, which is stamped by the characteristics of the situation determined by the group.

Thus in Gunkel we find once more tendencies which we described earlier as the driving impulses behind the intellectual questions of his time: the keen effort to see Israel consistently in the historical context of its environment; the striving to trace the upward development of phenomena in the history of religion until what is unmistakably and uniquely Israelite is attained; and the attempt to enter sympathetically into every individual stage of historical happening, to experience it directly, and in this way to understand it.

2. *Narrative Genres*

The saga

Since Gunkel's thesis that Genesis is a collection of sagas, the view has come to be generally accepted that a large part of the narrative material of the Old Testament goes back to sagas. Saga, therefore, is the name for a linguistic form which has its origin in the sphere of oral tradition. What is the mark of a saga?

(a) Linguistic form. The original saga is self-contained and forms a single unit of meaning. It is not dependent on other stories, but is capable of being understood directly and completely by the listener. The saga is therefore short, and its scope can be seen immediately. Gunkel says here:

The earliest narrators would not have been in a position to create more extensive works of art; nor would they have been able to demand of their hearers undiminished attention over days or even weeks. Rather, the ancients were content with quite small creations, taking up hardly a quarter of an hour. When the story then comes to an end, the hearer's imagination is also satisfied and his capacity for taking in the material is exhausted ... The briefer the saga, the more probable it is that it survives in early form (SAT I/1, p. 26).

In spite of its brevity, the saga has a firm structure. We find clearly depicted scenes: an exposition provides the preconditions for the subsequent events; this action is marked by complications which finally end in a solution. The saga generally comes to a peaceful close.

This concentration in the narrative is also displayed in the description of the people who appear. Only a few actors are involved, subsidiary characters hardly being mentioned. Two people appear in most scenes, often engaged in conversation. The main characters are not described elaborately with a great deal of differentiation; but a typical trait of character is brought out in a few strokes.

The chief characteristic of a story with this kind of structure is tension. The saga evokes tension and is concentrated on it; everything that does not serve this tension is omitted. All is directed towards the solution; so here we too must begin by asking about the saga's intent.

Hardly any detailed investigations have been carried out into the

linguistic form (in the narrower sense) associated with the genre of
saga (syntax, fixed formal elements, etc.). There is still much work to be
done here.

(b) The scope of the saga material.

(i) Family sagas. Particularly in the patriarchal narratives in
Genesis, we find stories which reflect life in the family or clan.
They deal with the fundamental events of this life: the birth
of the oldest son, relations between wife and concubine, rivalry
between brothers, quarrels with neighbouring groups, etc. In sagas
of this kind the historical dimension is completely lacking; events
take place on a timeless plane; we are dealing with things that
could happen again and again. Sagas of this kind still clearly show
that the family, which was rooted in the semi-nomadic civilization
of early times, both formed the horizon of life and was the pillar
that upheld it: the sagas are told in the family and in them we
meet fundamental family events; as yet the political and historical
element plays no part at all.

(ii) Tribal and heroic sagas. In the book of Judges, above all,
but in Joshua and in the books of Samuel as well, we come across
sagas which have as their theme the fate of a tribe or a similar
political unit. In this connection we must remember that the
Israelite tribes only grew up in the course of the settlement and in
its wake; their formation was due to the pressure of political
circumstances. In the framework of conflicts with other groups of
peoples, individual clans entered into a closer association with one
another. In the development of the tribe, political constellations and
events also played an essential part, and the outstanding leaders,
who came to the fore especially in times of testing for the tribe,
are at the centre of events. Here the sphere of history and politics
takes on prominence. We are dealing with historically localized
events – whether this localization is true or false in individual cases
is another matter.

(iii) Sagas about mankind as a whole. Particularly in the primaeval history in Genesis, we find sagas which deal with the destiny
of mankind as a whole. It also appears here that partly mythical
material has passed into saga form – material which really has to

do with the world and mankind in its totality (e.g. Gen. 11.1-9). On the other hand factors in the history of civilization affecting large groups of people have had the effect of forming sagas, and here the horizon – in accordance with the material – is wider than family or tribe.

(iv) Sagas about places and sanctuaries. A great many sagas have as their theme the founding of a sanctuary or sacred institution, or the explanation of some remarkable and well-known place. Stories of this kind will have been handed down by the groups who had to do with the particular sanctuary or place.

The sanctuary sagas occasionally reveal something of the religious ideas which were cultivated at the holy place in question (e.g. Gen. 28.10-20 E).

(v) Sagas about prophets. These stories grew up in the environment of prophecy. They reflect life within the groups of prophets which clustered round some great and revered teacher (Elisha, for example). The authority of the great prophets is celebrated and, at the same time, directions for the behaviour of the prophets are often given; in addition specifically prophetic theology frequently finds expression. Here the saga's simple linguistic form is often expanded.

(c) The function of the saga. What effect does the telling of a saga have? Why is it told? We may remember Gunkel's distinction between historiography and saga: in contrast to historiography, whose purpose is instruction, Gunkel defined the saga's intention as follows: 'It sets out to delight, to elevate, to inspire, to touch the heart.' On the other hand Gunkel also assumes that many sagas have a didactic function – for example when a local saga seeks to explain how a certain place came to have its name.

The saga, therefore, has its instructive, rational element. It communicates knowledge, for example about the origin of a people's own tribe, about its relations with neighbouring tribes, etc. But the instruction is viewed in emotional terms. The tension which is engendered and resolved in the process of telling binds the listener to the saga, allowing him to participate in the course of events. In this way the listener's attitude to a particular fact is moulded – and his attitude is again that of his group, whether it be the family, the tribe, the group of prophets, etc. To this extent the saga communicates an all-embracing, emotional and intellectual view of the world of the group from which it derives. In addition the saga of course has an entertaining, and often even an amusing, aspect.

(d) The expansion and development of the genre. Gunkel already established that the book of Genesis contains more than sagas which tell a story quite tersely in the ways we have described, reporting what has happened but confiding themselves to the essentials. There are also more extensive narratives. For Gunkel the clearest example is the story of Joseph, which is clearly distinguished from the short sagas by its extent (several chapters).

Here we find a multiplicity of long speeches, soliloquies, elaborate descriptions of situations and discussions of the ideas of the characters in the story. Here the narrator loves to repeat what has already been told in the form of discourse. A new taste apparently is developing and finding expression here. This new art does not content itself with relating the saga as briefly as possible, as the old one did; on the contrary, there is now a striving to elaborate it more luxuriantly and to develop its beauties, even if these are only by the way ... At the same time, the attention paid to the mind and heart of the individual is greatly intensified. There is now both the desire and the power to treat psychological problems (SAT I/1, pp. 33f.).

These detailed stories do not concentrate so much on outward events; they also observe the inner motivation of the actors, describing even less important features with elaborate art; Gunkel gives them the name *Novellen*. The different narrative method also leads to a change of emphasis in the intention of this linguistic form: the rational and instructive aspect comes more to the fore. The more relaxed narrative process allows more room for an appeal to the listener's intellectual, moral and aesthetic powers.

Another type, which is related to the *Novelle*, is the legend (or, to be more precise, the personal legend). The elaborate didactic style can be found here too; a holy figure (e.g. a priest or prophet) stands at the centre of the story and it is his saving or exemplary behaviour that is described.

In making a distinction between the simple, compressed form of the saga and the more extended genres, we should perhaps also presuppose a difference in the person of the narrator; in the simple sagas, which confine themselves to the essential elements, it is easily conceivable that any random person could take over the role of narrator; that is to say, we doubtless have popular narrative here. This is harder to conceive in the more extended genres, where much depends on the artistic description of details. Perhaps we could see here the hand of the professional story-teller, such as we find in the East even today. Gunkel's theory that the more extended genre simply represents a further development of the simple form is probably too sweeping a judgment.

(e) Development of the material (transmission history). In the transmission of oral narratives, the content is not rigidly fixed; it is variable. Thus persons and places, for example, can be changed; emphases in the content can shift; new aspects can be added, etc.

For example, the story of the 'peril of the mother of the race' can be found three times (Gen. 12.10ff.; 20; 26.7ff.). On two occasions Abraham and Sarah act as the couple, and on one occasion Isaac and Rebecca. Pharaoh appears once as the foreign potentate who threatens the wife, and a Canaanite village king, Abimelech, twice. Egypt is the scene of action once and Gerar twice. Is it still possible to establish which of this orally transmitted material is closer to the original? In this case it would be permissible to suppose that the tendency would be to replace less popular figures by well-known ones; thus one would have to think in terms of Isaac – Rebecca – Abimelech of Gerar; an analogous working hypothesis is used in textual criticism: the more difficult reading is the more probable.

More essential alterations arise when saga material is newly grouped or supplemented. Thus the material of two different sagas can be combined into a new saga, for example, and narrative motifs from folk-tale or myth are often introduced.

Finally, different sagas whose content is to some extent related have been brought together into a single complex – e.g. all the sagas in which Abraham plays a role, and all the Isaac sagas. A relationship has also been introduced between the Abraham sagas and the Isaac sagas: Abraham becomes Isaac's father (this should not be taken to be a historical fact, but is the result of the combination and reciprocal influence of saga complexes, i.e. a process in the history of their transmission). Isaac in his turn has Jacob assigned to him as a son, and so on. In connection with these first collections of sagas, which are centred on particular persons and sometimes also on particular places, Gunkel talks about 'saga cycles'.

Note on 'transmission history'. It is useful to confine the application of this term to the development of material at the oral stage, as outlined above. The term must be distinguished from the expressions 'redaction history' (see pp. 57f.) and 'tradition history' (see pp. 114f.). It is clear, moreover, that an examination of the development of form and material must take place simultaneously. Often tensions arise within a story in the course of a regrouping or expansion of the material; sometimes it is difficult to decide whether inconsistencies in the narrative or ideas are to be explained by the methods of literary criticism or on the basis of tradition history. On the connection between the approaches, see pp. 57f.

Genesis 16 may serve as an example. Here we meet the saga in the Yahwist version; it has its Elohistic parallel in 21.1-21. Verses 8-10 manage to reconcile the two stories; they tell why Hagar can be driven out twice; they are therefore to be assigned to the redactor who wove J and E together (RJE).

The saga begins as family history, with the problem of the chief wife's childlessness and the resulting conflict with the concubine, who is expecting a child. The conflict reaches its climax with the expulsion of Hagar. The expected solution follows: Hagar is saved – she finds a spring, an oasis. In a simple form of the saga we should expect a brief description of this solution.

Instead of that there is a complication: Yahweh appears in human form and talks to Hagar about the impending birth. With this the simple close has been abandoned, and the story is given a new development. Yahweh now employs a particular type of speech, which has its origin in the cult – that of the birth oracle. (A number of passages in the Old Testament and some outside it show where oracles of this kind have their setting: when a childless woman comes to the temple and complains there about her barrenness, she can hope for an oracle delivered by the priest, in roughly the following form: 'Fear not, behold you will conceive and bear a child ...' There follows an indication of the name the child is to be given. For examples in the Old Testament see I Sam. 1.1ff.; Judg. 13.2ff.; in addition Luke 1.5ff., etc.). This cultic genre thus appears as a narrative element within the saga. (Following Koch, we may call this a *component genre* in contrast to the *complex genre*, which determines the structure of the unit as a whole, cf. K. Koch, *The Growth of the Biblical Tradition*, 1969, pp. 23ff.).

The divine promise includes the name which the child is to receive. The Ishmael who is announced in this way is the tribal ancestor of the famous (or rather, notorious) predatory nomadic tribe. Ishmael is thus characterized by a tribal saying which also represents an independent genre. (Tribal sayings serve to bring out the characteristics of an alien tribe in a brief formula.) A favourite comparison was with an animal; the comparison is explained in a pregnant sentence. Cf. Gen. 49.3-27; Deut. 33.6-25, where the comparative stereotypes of the Israelite tribes are passed down; in part, admittedly, they are secondary formations and expansions.

The tribal saying added to the birth oracle here may originally have run:

Ishmael is a wild ass of a man,
his hand against every man, every man's hand against him.
He sets himself in the face of all his brothers.

There follows, finally, the link with a special place, which should probably be viewed as an oasis or shrine (vv. 13-15). The God who has saved Hagar and has revealed himself to her is called *'elrō'ī* and the place bears the name *be'er lahai ro'i*. The saga will therefore have been told in this region at a certain stage in its transmission.

Thus this saga is presented at an already highly complicated stage in the development of the genre and its transmission history. The fact of Sarah's childlessness links it with other Abraham sagas; the solution of the complications is not given in simple terms with the saving of Hagar, but is extended into the event of the child's birth; the divine discourse merges into the literary type of the birth oracle addressed to the barren woman; the boy, or the tribe which he represents, is qualified by means of a tribal saying; and finally a local shrine aetiology is added.

This is not the place to discuss the presumed prehistory of this saga material. The Israelite who heard it in the present version would at least remember the other Abraham sagas at the same time, and would be thinking simultaneously of the fate of Abraham's legitimate offspring, Isaac. Thus his attitudes would be given a particular stamp in a number of different respects; as regards the order of family life; as regards his relationship to the Ishmaelites, the enemy to whom he nonetheless felt himself related in a curious way; and finally above all as regards the action of Yahweh, which applied in the first place to his own race, but was also a saving action towards Ishmael.

Genres absent from the Old Testament

For an overall understanding of the Old Testament it is important to note the narrative genres that are missing, even though they are common coin among Israel's neighbours. Here special mention must be made of myth and the fairy tale (*Märchen*).

(a) Myth. A favourite definition of myth is 'a story about the gods', and in fact the characters who appear in myth are divine figures, whether the actions of an individual god are being described, or whether several gods are involved in an event. In the second case the action can be very complicated. The common characteristic of myth and saga is that they aim at a clearly definable outcome.

What marks myth out to a particular degree is its setting in the cult. In the archaic period the telling of myth was confined to its specific situation in worship; it was subject to a situation tabu. Sacred actions or rites were bound up with the sacred words. In certain circumstances the mythical happening was presented dramatically. Words and action formed an indissoluble whole, a ritual.

The intention of myth is to create reality. The conditions determined in myth form the world. Ritual has a power of creating order which is hardly comprehensible to the present-day mind; it gives the reason for the world and explains it as a whole or in partial spheres, both in man's consciousness and in external phenomena – although this division did not of course exist at all for ancient man.

The power of myth (one could term it a word with a magic effect) is founded on the fact that ancient man experiences himself (or his community, as the case may be) as the centre and starting point of his world. Through what he says and what he does he gives this world a certain structure; only in this way does it have meaning for him. Magic – i.e. the belief that one's own speech and actions have a powerful effect on the world – is a natural element in such an experience of the world. Such egocentricism, which developmental psychologists have described in similar terms in the case of the child, is largely alien to the grown-up in our civilization; he has learnt to a high degree to arrive at a decentralized way of looking at things – i.e. not to react on the basis of the direct perceptions of his own experience of the world. That is why it is so hard to understand the phenomena described here.

In myth the cultic community forms its world. The gods who play their part here are figures in whom the forces active in this world manifest themselves – forces in nature, in history, in society. In mythical happenings these forces arrive at a salutary balance. For instance, the Babylonian New Year myth (see pp. 41f.) constitutes the saving order in nature (activation of fertility) as well as in political and social conditions (warding off danger to the nation from within and without). In myth and ritual man exercised the greatest conceivable power: he forms his own destiny, together with that of the gods and of the whole world which surrounds him in a natural unity.

This genre is absent from the Old Testament. It may be – and it is even probable – that the Israelites, too, lived with myths in the early period. But in the body of sacred writings which crystallized out in Israel, myths have disappeared, except for minute remaining traces; whereas in Israel's environment they represent the category of religious language *par excellence*.

(b) The fairy tale. Like myth, the fairy tale belongs to archaic human thinking. Here too we meet supernatural notions (magic, etc.), and here too nature appears in animate form.

Unlike myth, the fairy tale enjoys no power to form reality. It handles the impressions of the world of magic with unbounded freedom. In many fairy tales wishful thinking plays an important part; it then appears as the point of crystallization for human desires and has a certain compensating function over against reality. Many fairy tales also serve to provide orientation in the ethical and moral sphere, in this respect resembling the saga; but the data remain quite vague: thus the fairy tale is rooted much more in the universal human condition than in a particular historical or social situation. A playful element frequently comes to the fore, and then pleasure in the unfolding of an unfettered fantasy is particularly clear.

There is not a single complete fairy tale in the Old Testament. This does not mean that no one told fairy tales in Israel; the reverse is probably true, for many sagas contain fairy-tale motifs (i.e. ideas typical of the fairy tale appear as elements in a saga). But in Israel the fairy tale did not prove to be a genre which would have been suited to express the religion of Yahweh; and incidentally the fairy tale is hardly ever a category of religious utterance anywhere else in the Ancient East either.

The transition to writing

Sooner or later texts which till then had only been passed on by word of mouth were committed to writing in Israel. We have already considered the written transmission of the text under the heading of literary criticism, but we can now look at it once more. For the questions thrown up by Gunkel now first drove scholars to enquire what lay behind the written form of the texts, and led to their arriving at oral units of speech. After that, on the one hand the sagas (for example) were traced through their development in the course of tradition back to their simplest recognizable form; on the other hand, the development of these stories was reconstructed from their origin down to the threshold of their written form. Thus once more we can enquire into the process of committal to writing and the history of written transmission which followed.

For every written text to which an oral prehistory can be attributed, the question arises as to the continuity between the oral and written stages of transmission. Two extreme possibilities are conceivable: either the writer fixes the linguistic unit in an unadulterated form, so that there is no difference between what is transmitted orally and what is transmitted in writing; or the writer gives a new form to the material at his disposal, bringing his own intention into play. Thus, for example, the saga in Gen. 16 which we have already mentioned seems to have remained largely unaltered when it was given fixed written form within J; whereas the Elohist, on the other hand probably liked to revise the fragments which came down to him in his own way (see pp. 22ff.).

The question of the procedure of an Old Testament writer also changes when we consider the extent to which oral transmission has already given the text its stamp. We must now ask first of all: Is the writer using traditional material here which has been passed down by word of mouth? Is the traditional material reproduced unchanged, or has it been altered? Or are we dealing with a passage which is the original creation of the writer?

Genesis 12.1-4a, 6-8 (J) is an example of a text which is not apparently stamped directly by any oral prototype. This story has none of the characteristics of a saga. Instead, it sketches programmatically the theological framework in which the Yahwistic stories take place. The themes of 'promise', 'guidance', 'blessing' and 'obedience' will of course come into play again and again. Here the Yahwist speaks directly and independently, and he formulates his programme. This does not mean that the headings of the programme were his own invention; they are not without prototypes either, but they are original in their literary form.

Units of this kind which are not 'traditional' are often called 'redactional' elements.

Note on redaction criticism. This expression has come to be used in New Testament research and can also be used in Old Testament exegesis. Redaction criticism follows the development of the text at its written stage. When an earlier oral stage can be assumed for a text, redaction criticism first describes how the oral material was treated when it was first committed to writing (framework, expansion, revision); it then goes on to investigate how the text, now written, was passed on again in writing and how it was remodelled.

Literary criticism, transmission history and redaction criticism. Literary criticism starts from the final result of the history of a biblical text. Because of disturbances in the text, contradictions, etc., it is compelled to enquire behind the text in its final form and to go into its history. The literary critic tries to separate out the individual strata in the text and finally to arrive at its original written form (Barth-Steck: 'the analytical process'). Now, the text may perhaps have an earlier oral history. To illuminate this – i.e. to penetrate behind the written form – is the task of transmission history. This, too, first of all proceeds analytically, enquiring after earlier and more recent elements in the sphere of oral transmission. But then the approach can be reversed: the development of a text is followed from its first recognizable beginnings (Barth-Steck: 'the synthetic process'). This approach can, of course, be prolonged beyond the threshold of writing; it is now called 'redaction history'. The synthetic process, which traces the development of the text through its oral and written transmission, has particular merit in that it is capable of depicting the way in which the text was interpreted anew in changed situations. The obscurities which may sometimes arise are no longer seen as disturbances to be eliminated (as is first the case in literary criticism); they are evaluated within the framework of an interpretative modification in the process of transmission. (A distinction is made here between 'transmission' and 'tradition' history which is explained on pp. 114f; English terminology tends to be less specific.)

The question of the relation between oral and written transmission is difficult to answer. In what way is the function of a text altered when it no longer lives in the relation between telling and hearing, but in that between writing and reading? Do oral and written tradition possibly run parallel at times? Does the writer think of his activity in a different way from the narrator? Does he give his work, say, a more individual note? At all events, the Old Testament writers remain anonymous – like the narrators before them. Subsequent 'redactors' freely revise the text, combining it with other texts, etc. The process of redaction in Deuteronomy may be recalled, where continuous work on the text is obvious. On the other hand, there are texts whose unmistakable originality is just as clear. The question of the continuity and the discontinuity between oral and written transmission cannot therefore be given a wholesale answer; it has to be investigated carefully in each text. That the transmission was more rigidly fixed at the stage when it was wholly written is obvious; on the other hand, there were new opportunities for recasting; the destruction of written texts and the compilation of new ones out of disparate elements – though of course these texts no longer seem compact and self-contained.

Scholarly opinion diverges as widely as it is possible to conceive in individual questions of this kind. How, for instance, is the Yahwist to be judged? Does he mark one stage within a continuous process of growth in the history of the tradition, which passes from the oral into the literary stage without any great hiatus? (This is the point of view particularly stressed by Martin Noth, *Überlieferungsgeschichte des Pentateuch*, 1948: he describes how the most varied narrative material is grouped round the main themes transmitted in the Pentateuch; how they grow together and so form a 'basic narrative', which is fixed in written or oral form. Here Gunkel's concept of 'saga cycles' is further developed. J and E are then in each case independent forms of the basic narrative G (*Grunderzählung*). However, they owe an enormous amount to G; it is hardly possible to lay hold of an independent trend, from which we could perhaps deduce the place, time and intention of the situation in which they came into being. In many cases Noth also reckons with a later expansion of J.) Today the majority of scholars stress the discontinuity between the oral stage of the transmission and J, above all following G. von Rad, 'The Problem of the Hexateuch', in *The Problem of the Hexateuch and Other Essays*, 1966, pp. 1ff. It is thought that the Yahwist had at his disposal only a brief confession of the saving history brought about by Yahweh (the 'short historical creed', see pp. 108ff.) together with a mass of unrelated material. The composition is then seen as J's original achievement; and accordingly an attempt is made to describe his literary and theological originality and to pinpoint it historically.

The form-critical approach which at the beginning applied principally to units of oral speech, can also be applied at the written stage of the transmission. Even now the units of text have their specific 'setting in life', i.e. specific occasions on which they are read or recited, their specific public, their specific intention – in short: their specific literary and sociological place. Of course we must note here that at the written stage individual features can acquire greater weight. Depending on the text, the individuality of the author has a greater or lesser influence on the embodiment of a form. (Corresponding differences can still be noticed today: trivial literature lives entirely from the laws of its genre, e.g. a bad detective story, or the 'births, marriages and deaths' in a daily newspaper have a maximum of 'genre' and a minimum of individuality.)

3. Genres of Cultic Poetry

The form-critical approach to cultic poetry – poetry which we find predominantly in the Psalter – divides up the material primarily according to the following aspects: either we have to do with individual psalms, where the relationship between the individual on the one hand and the community, as well as God, on the other is in the centre; or we are dealing with community psalms, which are an expression of the people in their relationship to God. The royal psalms have to some extent a position of their own. In the following section only the most important psalm types are named.

Individual psalms

(a) *The individual psalm of lament and the answering oracle of salvation.* The individual lament has as subject the man who for one reason or another no longer stands within the normal, healthful order of life and consequently sees himself as excluded from community with Israel and Yahweh. The reasons for this disintegration are generally summarized: the man who is praying is ill and suffering; he is oppressed by his enemies. The individual psalms can, according to circumstance, mention one aspect or the other; we also frequently encounter a combination of both themes. Sometimes the psalmist protests his lack of responsibility for his misfortunes; in other cases he is conscious of wrong-doing of his own which has ensnared him in his troubles.

These troubles culminate in the psalmist's death. In this connection we should not think of physical death, but of the condition of the person who is no longer at home in the community that forms his environment. For the Israelite of ancient times, life in isolation, in exclusion from the community, amounts to death; for the person who is making the lament, death is therefore the quality of his present situation.

Who are the enemies about whom individual laments talk so often and yet so vaguely? They seem to exercise a fearful power over the sufferer; they lie in wait for him, seek his life, etc. At all events, it can be said that everything which threatens the sufferer and tries to force him out of the community with Yahweh and the people has assumed concrete form in these enemies. They are probably not to be linked with particular people known to the psalmist. It is likely that in the background there is the idea of sorcerers who can exert an influence on men through their witchcraft – this is suggested by Mesopotamian exorcisms which can be compared with the psalms. The magic element had been largely eradicated in Israel. What remained was the knowledge of uncanny forces which were the enemies of life and which were capable of separating a man from the community and from God. Notions out of the collective psalms about 'enemies' have certainly had an influence as well.

The following elements mark the form of the individual lament. The principal feature is a description of the emergency, or an account of the way in which the troubles arose. These troubles are now brought to God in an invocation; lament becomes accusation (the marks of which are an address in the second person, a cry for help and demands that God should listen and see). In this way God is called to responsibility for the man's need. He is, after all, responsible for the ordered course of life and here the trouble lies. The lament turns into a plea.

Though the structure of the formal elements we have so far named is clear, astonishingly many individual laments are now characterized by a curious break. The section containing complaint and plea is often followed by a section in a mood of confidence. Here there is generally an acknowledgment of trust in Yahweh's help; the man praying expresses his certainty of this help (this is partly expressed in the perfect – Yahweh's help, like man's need earlier, therefore appearing as an established fact). With this a vow can be associated: the psalmist promises to offer a sacrifice and to praise Yahweh, once Yahweh's help has become clearly effective.

What is the explanation of this change of mood? Apparently the intention of the individual lament is to bring the sufferer once more into the community with his people and with Yahweh. Simply because the man praying can express his need in words in the cult, and is able to set it within the sphere of Yahweh's responsibility, this change has already taken place. Now Yahweh, as guarantor of the saving order, is called upon to make his righteousness prevail in the life of the worshipper as well; the acknowledgment of trust signalized the attitude of the man praying, who can reckon with Yahweh's vindication.

Lamentation in ancient Israel was probably in fact marked by an actual answer on the part of Yahweh. Apparently Yahweh's answer, uttered by a cultic official, had its place between lament/plea and the acknowledgment of trust.

We read an echo of a lament in Lam. 3.57: 'Thou didst come near when I called on thee; thou didst say, "Do not fear!" ' The concepts 'to call on' and 'to be near, to be far' are typical of the language of laments. Yahweh's answer evidently follows. In Ps. 12.1-4 there is a lament (even though it is not an especially typical one), Yahweh's answer appears in v. 6 and in v. 7 there is a reflection on the oracle.

Passages of this kind make it possible to reconstruct the whole process of lamentation and hearing.

Oracles of salvation are extant in a quite different text, in Deutero-Isaiah (e.g., Isa. 41.13f.; 43.1f.). They are marked by the introduction 'Fear not!', followed by the name of the person addressed. Then comes a development section, usually introduced by *ki*. It sometimes contains the confirmation that Yahweh has heard, that he helps, that he is near, etc. All the elements of the lament appear once more, but transformed into a positive sense.

The 'normal course' of ritual lamentation would therefore run as follows: lament/plea – answering oracle of salvation – acknowledgment of trust – possibly a vow made in thanksgiving. The reason for the change of mood would then be completely clear.

We need not assume, however, that every recital of an individual lament would have had its place in a liturgy of this kind. Otherwise it would hardly be conceivable that the elements sometimes do not appear in the 'normal' order. Often, too, only certain sections are emphasized (e.g., the lament over enemies, which is a prominent feature of 'psalms of revenge'; or the acknowledgment of trust, in 'psalms of confidence'; or the psalmist's insight into his own faults, which have led to his afflictions, in 'psalms of repentance'). In any case, the intention of the lament – reintegration into Yahweh's order of life – is preserved.

Examples: Ps. 13 is a typical psalm of lament: cf. vv. 1-4, which are the lament/plea (vv. 1 and 3 are addressed to Yahweh, vv. 2 and 4 describe the man's afflictions: pain, trouble, triumph on the part of his enemies). The transformation follows: v. 5 brings the acknowledgment of trust. Ps. 54 has a vow of sacrifice and praise. Ps. 35 is a lament over the enemy. Ps. 23 is a psalm of confidence.

(b) The individual song of thanksgiving. Through the vow, there is sometimes an indirect reference in individual laments to the festival of thanksgiving: when the promise made by the oracle of salvation has taken definite form in the sufferer's attitude to life – when, that is to say, the author of the lament sees himself again integrated into communion with people and God – the time has come to seek the temple once more,

The formal characteristics of the hymn of thanksgiving correspond clearly to its function. Main elements are: a retrospective
glance at the troubles which the psalmist has endured (the language of the individual lament of course appears at this point);
mention of the intervention and saving help of Yahweh, which
gives the psalmist's destiny a favourable turn: and finally praise of
God.

It is noticeable that the individual song of thanksgiving is
frequently addressed to two different quarters: on the one hand to
God, and on the other to members of the community in which the
man who is giving thanks sees himself once more accepted. Hence
the following formal elements, for example, are found side by side:
'I will bless Yahweh' (Ps. 34.1) and 'Magnify Yahweh with me'
(Ps. 34.3); the call to praise God is addressed both to the person
giving thanks and to his companions. The person who has been
saved tells those who are with him of his distress and his deliverance ('ªsappᵉrā, e.g., Ps. 9.1); in this way they too are drawn into
the praise of God, recognizing and acknowledging Yahweh as the
God of their order of salvation and their order of life.

It must also be remembered that the person who has been delivered offers a sacrifice, a *zebah* (cf. Ps. 27.6; 54.8). This is a sacrifice
which ends in a common meal. In the case of the feast of thanksgiving, the relations and perhaps friends of the one who has been
delivered will have taken part. This makes it completely clear that
the person giving thanks has been once more accepted into his
circle of society: he eats and drinks with his companions in the
presence of the deity.

Community psalms

(a) Hymns. The hymn, the praise of God, marks Israel's regular
worship. Normally Israel feels able to express its experience that
Yahweh makes his saving order prevail on Israel's behalf; the
reaction that follows this experience is the praise of God.

The hymn has been preserved in Israel in two basic forms: it
either contains an account of God's acts, which have led to the
constitution of the saving order; or it describes the nature of God, as
this has been manifested since time immemorial in the order of

salvation. The two basic forms must be carefully distinguished: each of them has a different meaning for Old Testament theology and, in the sphere of religious history, each has a different setting.

The first of the two basic forms is to be found in the *imperative hymn*. The formal characteristics are laid down as follows: the introduction is formed by a plural imperative containing a call to praise God. The demonstrative particle *ki* follows immediately and points to the subject of the ensuing praise. The shortest and oldest example of the form is the Song of Miriam, a hymn in response to the deliverance of the exodus which we can probably assign to Israel's earliest cult:

I will sing to Yahweh, for he has triumphed gloriously; the horse and his rider he has thrown into the sea.

The subject of the praise here is a historical event which has become of basic importance for Israel's existence and self-understanding, and which is praised as Yahweh's act.

The individual elements of the genre can be extended. Both the imperative (and the people addressed by it) and the part of the hymn which gives its content and its reason for it, are frequently developed in considerable detail. The genre retains its vitality down to the late Israelite period. Some post-exilic expressions of the imperative hymn contain an actual list of the facts of salvation-history (e.g., Pss. 105; 107). In other examples, actual events are not named but Yahweh's actions in history are described in summary form (e.g., Pss. 96 and 98, which are pre-exilic).

In the cult, therefore, the events are remembered through which Yahweh gave Israel's life its impress – particularly in its historical dimension. Here is one root of those outlines of salvation history which are so characteristic of many Israelite domains.

The imperative hymn is contrasted with the *hymn in participial style*. This is marked by the characteristic string of participles which describe the being and behaviour of God, which can continually be experienced anew (e.g. Job. 5.9ff.). There is no longer any complete hymn of this genre in the Old Testament. The genre therefore fell into disuse in the course of Israel's cultic history and became mingled with the elements derived from other genres. In particular, the introduction characteristic of hymns of this kind is not known to us.

Still, some passages in Amos probably allow us to deduce what the characteristic conclusion of hymns of this kind was. Here, too, there are participial lists (as there are in several other books as well) – of course we are not dealing here with genuine sayings of Amos. At the end comes the cry: 'Yahweh, the God of hosts is his name!' (Amos 4.13; similarly 5.8; 9.6). Perhaps this formula is a typical conclusion to the hymn in participial style; a summary stresses that all the activities described through the participles belong to Yahweh.

The hymn in participial style is distinguished from the imperative hymn in content as well as in form. Here the hymn is concerned with certain divine behaviour which recurs in a typical way, not with the account of unique events. Correspondingly, the participles refer principally to God's activity in creation and nature, though they go on to embrace his typical behaviour towards men as well.

The fact that the hymn in participial style did not endure as a type in Israel shows that no central importance was assigned to it. Its outstanding formal element – the list of participles – became a linguistic element in other types, including the imperative hymn. The reporting, narrating and preserving of historically unique and irreplaceable elements was an aspect which obviously had more weight for Israel's hymnody than the description of typical and timeless modes of divine behaviour.

This observation is supplemented by a finding that belongs to the history of religion. Hymns with participial lists are a common form of speech among Israel's neighbours. The subject-matter too corresponds almost entirely; the same behaviour is attributed to Babylonian gods, for instance, as is ascribed to Yahweh. This leads us to a possible explanation for what we suspect was the final formula of the participial lists: the characteristics which were generally attributed to the gods in the ancient East are claimed pre-eminently for Yahweh. The imperative hymn, on the other hand, has only remote analogies in its environment; it is peculiar to Israel. This also explains why it survived as a genre throughout the whole of Israel's development.

(b) Laments. When the entire community's way of life is in danger

– when, that is to say, Yahweh's order as a whole is called in question – it is an occasion for the collective lament. We should think here, in concrete terms, of the most varied threats to the nation: natural disasters, famine, danger in time of war, etc. In these cases a day of national mourning was proclaimed (Hebrew: *qārā' sūm*, 'to proclaim a fast day'). The service of lament took place in the temple, and it is here that the collective lament found expression.

Like the individual lament, the collective genre also knows elements of lamentation (the description addressed to Yahweh, of the threatening situation) and the plea for Yahweh's intervention. Here the enemies, who are often named, are to be seen as being the political opponents who are threatening Israel's existence.

This is generally followed by a retrospective glance at God's saving order, which had previously been in force but now seemed to be in danger. Here we find historical events mentioned in the first place (the central subject-matter of the imperative hymns, cf. for example Pss. 80; 44), but there are also pointers to God's acts in nature as well as mythical reminiscences (the main subject of the hymns containing participial series; cf. e.g. Ps. 74).

The lament and the retrospect of the earlier order of salvation are contrasted with one another. The accusation is levelled at the saving order, just as it is in the individual lament. Because it has become questionable in general, it must be called to remembrance in particular terms. God is appealed to to uphold his order and is charged with his will towards salvation, which has continually been experienced in the past.

We occasionally find a declaration of trust on the part of the people, based on this will of Yahweh's towards salvation, as it is known from the past (e.g., Ps. 44.5ff.; this single element by itself can determine a whole psalm, e.g. Ps. 46).

The divine oracle seems to have played a central part in the collective lament, as it did in the individual one. There is a reference to one in Ps. 85.9, for example (though no clear date can be assigned to the psalm). After the retrospect and the lament, we find the remark: 'I will hear what God will speak; God, Yahweh, he surely speaks of salvation (*kī yᵉdabber šālōm*)!' Cries of *šālōm* are familiar from the Old Testament prophets (Micah, Jeremiah and Ezekiel take a critical attitude towards them, cf. Micah 3.5; Jer. 6.14; 8.11; Ezek. 13.10. A cry of salvation of this kind survives in Isa. 57.19). In this case God's order of šālōm was apparently brought to mind and put into force through the prophetic call. In addition, we must also suppose that there was prophetic intercession.

Royal psalms

Some of the psalms centre upon the person of the king. Because the king bears responsibility for the whole nation, the nation's fate is also an indirect theme in psalms of this kind. The king is referred to in the third person, that is to say a cultic official acts as spokesman. In all cases the royal psalms deal with the king's relationship to God, to the people and to the enemy – which shows how close these psalms are to the collective psalms in function. Intercession for the king appears to have played an essential role (cf. Pss. 20; 21; 72), although their situation in the cult is difficult to determine precisely. Psalms 2 and 110 contain forms to be used on the king's accession or enthronement; Psalm 45 is an epithalamium.

Psalms for special festivals

Some of the psalms suggest that they belong to particular festal occasions. The difficulty is that it is only from psalms of this kind that the nature of the festival and the course it took can be reconstructed, since information about the ancient Israelite festival cult is not found anywhere else in the Old Testament. In Psalm 132 a festival connected with the ark of the covenant seems to be indicated and in Psalm 47 a festival celebrating the enthronement of Yahweh; Psalm 14 too probably also reflects some festival ceremony. Do all these psalms (and perhaps some others as well) belong to the one festival?

Psalms where the cry *yhwh malak* appears are often termed enthronement psalms (Pss. 93; 96; 97; 99; in addition *mālak 'elōhīm* appears in Ps. 47). The only thing which these different psalms have in common is the phrase, and no attempt should be made to construct a unified literary type out of it. Moreover, with the exception of Psalm 47, no ritual proceeding seems to be outlined in these psalms (cf. pp. 98f. below).

The departure from unified genres

(a) Elements drawn from different genres. A great many of the psalms in the Old Testament can no longer be assigned to a *single* literary type on the basis of formal characteristics. Elements derived from different types are mixed, becoming original compositions. Of course the characteristics of the various genres had never been rigid rules; the order of particular elements and their respective importance was not fixed in the individual laments, for example; we have already seen in some detail that there was a close relationship between the individual lament and the individual song of thanksgiving; and it is not unusual for the praise of God in the song of thanksgiving sometimes to display hymnic diction. But in some psalms the mixture of elements derived from one genre or another goes considerably further. In these cases obligation towards a particular genre is obviously hardly felt any more. The psalmists begin to handle the most varied elements of form and concept with individual freedom, in order to create from them their own unique poetry.

Without doubt, psalms of this kind also played their part in the cult. In spite of that, we often have the impression that these poems have to some extent detached themselves from cultic use – this is true, for example, of the acrostic psalms (psalms where the first letters of the verses are in alphabetical order); here the appeal seems to be to the reader's eye rather than to the ear of the congregation. Summing up, we could describe this process as follows: these poems are determined less by the linguistic situation of the community than by the individuality of the psalmist. It may be said in general that during the late Israelite period weight shifts with increasing clarity towards the more individual composition, especially after individualism had acquired greater influence through the exile (cf. pp. 132f.).

For example, in Psalm 92 we first find the influence of the opening of the imperative hymn (v. 2) – but here it is transposed in reflective terms

into a general maxim. The *kī*, introducing the development, appears in
v. 5; the reason takes the form of the individual song of thanksgiving.
The expression of astonishment in v. 6 again derives from the hymn,
and so on. What is remarkable is the reflection which continually
permeates the traditional elements.

(b) The intervention of modes of thought alien to the cult. In the
case of Psalm 92, we suggested that the element of reflection plays
a determining part. This can be noticed in many other psalms of
this kind as well. Moreover, it is clear that *wisdom thinking* determines this reflection (cf. pp. 77ff.). A whole series of psalms can be
termed 'wisdom psalms'. This does not mean that they are a clearly
definable literary type; but they are poems in which the wisdom
element has become dominant, although in most cases one can
recognize formal elements deriving from cultic types. In Psalm 37,
for example, the language of the individual lament is obvious
again and again, but it has been absorbed into wisdom exhortation
and reflection. Whether poems of this kind had a 'setting in the
cult' is very questionable; they more probably served non-cultic
edification and instruction.

In some psalms of this kind the law (*tōrāh*) is the subject of the
reflection. Here *tōrāh* has become the centre of divine revelation;
it is interpreted in terms of wisdom and in cultic categories (cf.
for example the acrostic Psalm 119). For the origin of the term
tōrāh see p. 77.

(c) The evolution of individual ideas. It is understandable that in
poetry of this kind, which handles elements from the genres extremely freely, new and unconventional ideas should appear. Thus
these psalms can view and come to terms with, say, the problem of
death in a different way from the classical individual lament.
'Death' is no longer simply exclusion from the community, because
the community has ceased to make use of its integrating function
as before; death has now turned into a much more individual
problem. We should read Psalm 73.23ff. in this context:

Nevertheless I am continually with thee;
    thou dost hold my right hand.

Thou dost guide me with thy counsel,
    and afterward thou wilt receive me to glory (text emended).
Whom have I in heaven but thee?
    And there is nothing upon earth
that I desire besides thee.
    My flesh and my heart may fail,
But Yahweh is my rock and my portion (text emended).

Clearly the subject here is physical death, which cannot be abolished
by any community. Consequently a religious motif intervenes here
which is otherwise alien to the psalms – the motif of 'ascension'. This
is widespread in the ancient East, and in Israel as well (Elijah, in II
Kings 2.1ff; Enoch, in Gen. 5.24). The poet uses it here in a completely
original way, in order to express his personal 'togetherness' with God,
which even death cannot shake.

In this way, out of the conventional language and thought which
is closely bound up with the formal language of the genres, a
religious poetry has evolved which bears the stamp of the individual. The poem of Job also belongs within this context of
literary history.

4. Genres of Law

The essential impulse for the form-critical investigation of Old
Testament law was given by Albrecht Alt, whose 'The Origins of
Israelite Law' appeared in 1935 (ET in *Essays on Old Testament
History and Religion*, 1966, pp. 3-77). The different genres which
are recognizable within the codes of Old Testament law are determined according to their function in the legal life of ancient Israel. Alt
arrives at a basic distinction between law that is formulated in
'casuistic' terms and law that is formulated 'apodictically'.

Casuistic law

The distinctive formal characteristic [of casuistic law] is that it is
invariably introduced by an objective conditional clause beginning
'If ...'. Throughout, all those who are concerned in the case under
discussion are spoken of in the third person – the person who commits

the act and his adversary, but also the judge and God himself.... The syntactical construction of the laws, however, is invariably based on the sequence of the protasis and apodosis of a conditional sentence, in that order, and the difference between the main cases in question and subsidiary cases is expressed by the use of two different conjunctions for the conditional clause, the stronger *kī*, 'granted' or 'supposing that', and the weaker *'im* 'if' (*Essays,* p. 89).

This clearly describes the formal characteristics: the conditional clause contains a fact, which can be differentiated; the main clause contains the legal consequence. (For example, in Ex. 21.20f. the circumstance, introduced by *kī*, and the first differentiation are that someone strikes his slave and he dies immediately.) From this the legal consequence is deduced that the man who has committed the act is to be punished. A second differentiation of the circumstance, introduced by *'im*, is that the slave goes on living for a time and only dies later; the legal consequence is that the man is not punished.

How is the *Sitz im Leben* – the setting in life – to be determined?

Such laws can have been used only in the exercise of normal jurisdiction. In their conditional clauses the description and definition of a particular case set the pattern for the trial, while the judgment would be based on the provisions as to the penalty in the main clauses, wherever the same or a closely similar charge was under discussion (*Essays,* p. 91).

This jurisdiction had its place in every village; it was carried out by the elders, who were called within the gate (*ša ar*) either to come to a decision there or to authorize a public transfer for jurisdiction (cf. for example the description in Ruth 4.1ff.).

In a number of characteristic passages the deity plays a part – and always when a matter cannot be decided because of contradictory statements (e.g. Ex. 22.8ff.). The deity is approached for advice in naming the innocent person or the guilty one. That is to say, a divine judgment is sought (ordeal). We must assume that the elders, together with the parties in the dispute, went to the local shrine, put the question 'guilty or not guilty?' to the representative of the deity and received an oracular answer – probably an oracle derived from the simple drawing of lots. Similar proceedings are known outside Israel as well.

After these discussions Alt asks in what civilization this kind of legal precept originated; his conclusion is that it is to be found in *Canaanite* civilization. It is therefore not a specifically Israelite phenomenon; it is common to both Israel and her neighbours. Accordingly Alt fails to find any specific consciousness of Israel as a people in these legal precepts; their content simply presupposes the cultural conditions of a village or city civilization, such as was indigenous to Canaan. The same stylistic characteristics can be found in non-Israelite legal codes, e.g., in the Code of Hammurabi. Where God is mentioned, the proper name Yahweh never appears, but always the neutral *'elōhîm*. The conclusion to be drawn from all this is that, in the framework of their absorbtion of Canaanite culture, the Israelites also took over this legal form, without remodelling it in accordance with their national consciousness and their own religious sense.

Apodictic law

(a) *Alt's hypothesis*. Alt finds legal precepts in the Old Testament which have a completely different form from the casuistic law we have just discussed. Exodus 21.15 is one example: 'Whoever strikes his father or his mother shall be put to death.' Legal precepts of this kind are remarkable for their close, terse formulation; there are only short main clauses. Moreover, there is no differentiation between different nuances in the facts; above all, no attention is paid to the subjective attitude of the wrongdoer to the act he has committed; for example, there is no differentiation between murder and manslaughter, which is a matter of course for casuistic law.

We find series of apodictic laws, all demanding the death penalty for particular offences (*mōt yūmāt* sentences), in Ex. 21.12, 15-17; the stylistic form is occasionally found outside this series as well. In content these sentences are marked by the fact that they

deal to an overwhelming degree with matters which the casuistic law never mentions, and with which from its secular nature it could have

no concern. They deal in part with the sacred realm of man's relations
with the divine ... For the rest, they deal with sacred areas within the
community, and particularly, though not in every case, with the family.
Religion, morality and law are all included without any distinction,
for everything is referred to the unconditional will of God; so that for
every breach of the law only the severest punishment is possible, the
personal extermination of the evil doer (*Essays*, pp. 113f.).

Apodictic law thus has to do directly with Yahweh's will; this
explains its unqualified validity and it is to this, again, that the close
formulation also corresponds.

According to Alt, linguistic features of a very different form
also belong to apodictic law. First of all comes the series of crimes
laid under a curse (Deut. 27.15-26). Formally speaking, these are
again main clauses, which are introduced by *'arūr*, 'cursed', naming
the doer of the deed in a participle. The people solemnly ac-
knowledges the curse in a confirmatory 'amen'. According to Alt,
offences are also involved here which have to do with the sacred
sphere – those which are difficult to discover and hence are
hardly accessible to human punishment. The curse is to fall on
the hidden wrongdoer and to cut him off from the community of
Israel.

Finally, according to Alt, a third linguistic form belongs to
apodictic law, i.e., formulations similar to the commandments in
the Decalogue. These are marked by a form of address in the
second person and a negation (*lō'* + imperfect). The presupposition
here is that originally all the commandments of this kind were
negative in form; the positive commandments – the hallowing of
the sabbath and the honouring of parents, for example – would
accordingly be secondary recastings. The direct address is an element which is completely missing in casuistic law; the directness
of the apodictic legal claim contrasts sharply with the detached lists
of differentiated facts and situations and their appropriate legal
consequence.

Alt, then, assigns legal precepts of extremely varied linguistic
form to apodictic law. The common features are seen as the formation of series, the absolute character of the injunctions, the linguistic
compression, and the bond with Yahweh's will. How can such

legal precepts be placed in the legal life of ancient Israel? What is their 'setting in life'?

We have no need to invent such a context, for it is provided in the tradition, itself, wherever a list of apodeictic laws is set in descriptive framework. A particularly clear instance is the setting of the curses in Deut. xxvii: this list is presented as being delivered orally by the leviti-cal priests to the whole people, assembled in the great natural am-phitheatre between Ebal and Gerizim in the Vale of Shechem; the people take each curse upon themselves with a cry of 'Amen'. The apodeictic law provides the central text for sacred action involving the whole nation, and those who proclaim it are the mouthpiece of Yahweh, the levitical priests ... (*Essays*, p. 125).

When other series use 'thou' as the form of address, they therefore address the people as a whole. This sacral act would have taken place every seven years, at the Feast of Tabernacles (Deut. 31.9).

According to Alt, this feast had a constitutive significance for Israel. Every seventh year the cultivation of the fields ceased, and debts and legal obligations were cancelled; Yahweh claims his rights of ownership and lordship in Israel, and helps every Israelite to return to his clan and the land of his inheritance.

But if the purpose of this unique and peculiarly Israelite institution was the return to normal community after the disturbances and false develop-ments of the previous six years, then the proclamation of the apodeictic – the specifically Israelite – law at the Feast of Tabernacles, that is, at the beginning of the seventh year, has a precise and relevant purpose. It signifies the recalling of the people to the ideals on which its existence is based, a renewed pledging of every member of the nation to the will of Yahweh, without which the welding of the tribes into a national unity could not have come about, nor could endure. Hence, although the expression may not be one that is in use, the origin of the proclama-tion of the apodeictic law, placing an obligation on the whole nation at the Feast of Tabernacles, is a regular *renewal of the covenant* between Yahweh and Israel of which they were conscious as the very source of their national life (*Essays*, pp. 128f.).

The apodictic law thus had its setting in a cultic ceremony which was constitutive for Israel from its earliest period – the feast of the renewal of the covenant (see further p. 108). The question of whether the genre of the law can be traced back still further, to the remote antiquity of Yahweh religion in the desert, is pursued by Alt only in a few suggestions; but an origin of this kind seems to him probable.

(b) Alt's hypothesis: problems. In recent times doubts have been increasingly expressed about Alt's conception. Here we can only indicate the general direction taken by the critical development of his theses, or by contrary theories.

1. Perhaps Alt's fundamental weakness is that he claims three different basic linguistic forms for a single literary type. Most of the investigations on the subject then concentrate on one of these three basic forms.

2. How is apodictic law bound to Yahweh's will?

Elliger has investigated a series of commandments extant in Lev. 18 which has the following constant form: 'Thou shalt not have sexual intercourse with X (here different grades of female relationship are inserted).' By means of a number of transmission-historical considerations, he reconstructs a series of ten commandments, i.e. a decalogue. The selection of female relations with whom the person addressed is to have no sexual intercourse reflects the social grouping in Israel's early, semi-nomadic civilization. The person addressed is the male adult, who is forbidden to have sexual intercourse with the wives of the men who live with him in the group formed by the clan (blood relationship plays no part). From this it can be deduced that commandments of this kind were in fact already known to pre-Israelite groups before the constitution of Israel as a nation. There is, however, no question of a bond with Yahweh's will.

3. Are the apodictic commandments really peculiar to Israel?

Gerstenberger in particular stresses that the rules of this kind were known not only in Israel but in the Semitic world generally. In places – and sometimes within other ancient Eastern legal codes as well – formularies are to be found which one could call apodictic (adopting the usual terminology of Old Testament exegesis).

4. Is a cultic setting for the various apodictic commandments probable?

Only the *'arūr* sentences clearly indicate a cultic framework for the proclamation of the law. Moreover, this is a late text and there are therefore no problems in drawing conclusions from it about the early Israelite period; many scholars even see the cultic setting as a literary fiction. In the case of the other forms, the question is still more difficult to answer. H. Schulz assumes that the *mōt yūmāt* sentences derive from the cultic legislative community (which he distinguishes from the secular legal community); he looks for the origins in the early period of tribal organization. But it is as impossible to talk about a specifically cultic setting here as it is in the case of the decalogue commandments already mentioned. At the same time, it is worth considering whether what were originally non-cultic commandments did not, at an earlier or later period in Israel, turn into divine law, proclaimed in the cult.

5. Are these sentences of apodictic law really *law* at all? That is to say, are they formulations primarily aimed at jurisdiction, the enforcement of the law, etc.? Or is the aim of the apodictic decrees the much more comprehensive sphere of ethical education, a general training in the norms of behaviour?

Series of apodictic rules like those which Elliger has worked out as being the basic form of Lev. 18 suggest that formularies of this kind are not really law; they are a fixing of the norms of behaviour in particular spheres of life. In this case the setting of these formularies would have to be sought, not in the legal sphere, but in education and instruction. From where do the apodictic rules take their unqualified authority, if the bond with Yahweh's will was not originally constitutive for that authority? Here it is usual to point to the unqualified validity of the archaic tribal order and its norms, which would have been expressed in a series of apodictic commandments of this kind, expounded and supervised by the elders, the exponents of that tribal order. Of course we are only familiar with the normative consciousness of the ancient tribal constitution from reconstructions – e.g. from the apodictic commandments.

If it is assumed that the apodictic rules had their primary function in instruction, then the question naturally arises of their relation to wisdom. Have the admonitory maxims of wisdom and the apodictic rules the same root? Is it possible to establish a different function within the framework of instruction for prohibitions with *'al* from those with *lo'*? See further pp. 79f. below.

Priestly instruction

Priestly instruction (*tōrāh*) could also be described as legal precepts, though admittedly it deals only with a quite specific sphere, namely the cult. It is the priest's task to distinguish between sacred and secular, between unclean and clean, between what the cultic law permits and what it forbids. This is of the greatest importance for the cultic proceedings in the temple. The priest gives his decision as one commissioned by Yahweh; the *tōrāh* therefore consists formally in a brief saying of Yahweh's, which can be given different forms. Either a command or a prohibition is given, addressed directly to the person affected; or we have a short statement whose subject is the pronouncement of Yahweh's will; or a brief statement suffices, e.g. a judgment as to whether something is clean or unclean, sacred or secular ('cultic declaratory judgments').

We may assume that the priests issued these instructions in the sanctuary. In the exercise of their office, they no doubt had to give various directions to the laity, who had assembled for the cultic proceedings; often enough they will also have been confronted with real questions from the laity about cultic matters; the answer would then take the form of a *tōrāh*.

We have evidence that the issuing of *tōrāh* was a priestly function in Jer. 18.18; Ezek. 7.26. For the priestly duty to instruct as to what was clean and what was unclean, cf. Ezek. 22.26. For a layman's enquiry and the priest's directions, cf. Hag. 2.11-13.

The concept of *tōrāh* changed greatly in the course of Israelite history. In priestly circles the meaning of the term first developed in the direction of priestly knowledge *per se* – i.e. not merely concrete directions to a layman. Later it took on a more general meaning and became the expression for Yahweh's revelation *per se*. This is so, for example, in the psalms we have already mentioned which reflect and meditate on Yahweh's revelation (cf. pp. 68f.; also pp. 122f.).

5. Genres of Wisdom

Old Testament terms

The Old Testament names a third authority – and perhaps even profession – alongside the priest and prophet, the wise man (*ḥāḵām*). His characteristic utterance is called counsel (*'ēṣā*), cf. Jer. 18.18;

Ezek. 7.26. The *'ēṣā* is evidently an oral saying; its special function
and intention are again a matter for enquiry.

In the Old Testament the term for the wisdom saying is *māšāl*.
Generally speaking, this means a maxim which can frequently be
repeated – it can be a proverb, a figure of speech, a satirical poem,
and so forth. The use of *māšāl* is not therefore confined to wisdom
sayings, though it does fit, as they are meant for use on more than a
single occasion. *Māšāl* therefore relates to the repeated application
of the wisdom sayings and *'ēṣā* to their function.

Simple and extended forms

One basic form of wisdom speech is the *proverb*, a statement
consisting of a single term. An example can be found in Ezek.
16.44: 'Like mother, like daughter.' Here the verb *mšl* is used, and
the proverb is applied by Ezekiel to Jerusalem; the city is symbolically called the daughter of a Hittite, both daughter and mother
being accused of an inclination towards incest.

In the sphere of wisdom, the proverbs are expanded into at least
two-member *aphorisms*, in which the rules of *parallelism* play an
essential role. Here the different possibilities of the relation between
two parallel terms must be noted (chiefly synonymous and antithetical parallelism, and more rarely so-called synthetic 'parallelism', in which the second term contains a development instead
of a parallel):

Pride goes before destruction,
    and a haughty spirit before a fall (Prov. 16.18: synonymous).
One man pretends to be rich, yet has nothing;
    another pretends to be poor, yet has great wealth (Prov. 13.7; anti-
thetical).

It is quite conceivable that these two proverbs correspond to what
were originally single-member proverbs, and have been expanded
through a synonymous or an antithetical parallel member.

It seems that earlier Israelite wisdom consists almost exclusively
of individual proverbs in this parallel form. As against this, the
combination of two or more units probably represents a further
development. Longer compositions, which have a literary character,
are to be found in Prov. 1-9; they are probably to be judged as a

late product of Israelite wisdom; clear formal rules are no longer recognizable.

One section of the book of Proverbs (22.17 – 23.11), which goes back to Egyptian sources, has something to tell us here. As a rule four terms appear as a unit of thought, sometimes more. In all cases, however, the Egyptian text has been shortened. From this it may perhaps be deduced that at the period when these proverbs were composed in Israel, the proverbial unit was in principle still brief – hence the shortening of the Egyptian model. Proverbs 22.17ff. is probably to be assigned to the period of the monarchy; Egyptian influences have made a substantial contribution to the formation of the extended forms.

The aims of wisdom discourse

One of the primary intentions of wisdom discourse is to *establish* a fact of experience and to summarize it in a descriptive way. Of course there are contradictory experiences which confirm one another by their very discrepancy. The reflection of them in proverbial form is therefore contradictory. To take an example:

The ransom of a man's life is his wealth,
  but a poor man – truly he hears rebuke! (Prov. 13.8)
A rich man's wealth is his strong city,
  and like a high wall – in his imagination (Prov. 18.11: RSV alternative reading).

Contrasting experiences (that riches are generally capable of defending a man against all kinds of unpleasantness, but that this is not invariably so) are in each case summed up and established as a fact in aphoristic statements (there are parallels for both, cf. Prov. 10.15; 14.20 compared with 11.28). Wisdom is further concerned to *order* its experience. Perhaps the clearest case of the genre-like development of this character of wisdom in the Old Testament is to be found in the *number proverb*. To take an example:

Under three things the earth trembles;
  under four it cannot bear up:
a slave when he becomes a king,
  and a fool when he is filled with food;
an unloved woman when she gets a husband,
  and a maid when she succeeds her mistress (Prov. 30.21).

Here four circumstances are linked together which endanger the functioning of the social order in some way or other – it can be the state or marriage that is in question. The number proverb first sums up what is common to the phenomena which are afterwards listed, giving the number of the things mentioned; then follows the description of every individual phenomenon.

An essential function of wisdom discourse is *admonition*. The admonition can be positive or negative.

Hearken to your father who begot you,
> and do not despise your mother when she is old (Prov. 23, 22: synony-
> mous parallelism).

In many cases a reason follows (in positive exhortations generally introduced by *kī*); in a negative exhortation, a prohibition, there is often a warning (with *pen*) about the consequences of the offence.

The admonitory proverb has been the subject of considerable discussion in recent years. Its distribution within wisdom literature is striking. It appears above all in sections which are strongly influenced by Egyptian wisdom or have even been translated from Egyptian; otherwise the proverb that establishes a fact is far more common. In Egypt, on the other hand, the admonitory proverb is by far the most common form of wisdom discourse. This does not exactly allow us to draw the conclusion that Israel's admonitory proverb is a type borrowed from Egypt (we find admonitory proverbs e.g. in Babylon as well, though not in very great number), but it is obvious that the Egyptian influence also affects the preference for a particular form of discourse.

W. Richter has investigated the relationship between apodictic commandments and admonitory sayings. The verbal difference is that the apodictic commandments are given their negative form with *lo'*, the admonitory sayings with *'al* (Richter talks about prohibitive and veti-tive forms, following Akkadian grammar; the first form represents a negation of the cohortative present, the second a negation of the jussive). The apodictic prohibitions are originally supplied with no justification; the admonitory sayings generally have one. The content of apodictic prohibitions and admonitory sayings can often be shown to be similar – most clearly in Deut. 19.14 on the one hand and Prov. 22.28; 23.10 on the other. This means that the norms generally accepted among the people, which are expressed in apodictic commandments, continue to be observed in wisdom – just as wisdom continued to recognize proverbial insights. The admonitory sayings are therefore to be viewed as an independent type of Israelite wisdom discourse; their content is derived in part from apodictic rules and they received considerable stimulus from Egyptian wisdom in both significance and content.

A fourth basic function of wisdom discourse is to pose *questions*. These may take the form of riddles (Hebrew *ḥīdā*). By means of riddles a wise man's knowledge can be tested (this is what the queen of Sheba does with Solomon, according to I Kings 10.1). This procedure often appears as a motif in fairy tales. A riddle with its answer is to be found in Prov. 23.29f.:

Who has woe? Who has sorrow?
  Who has strife? Who has complaining?
Who has wounds without cause?
  Who has redness of eyes?
Those who tarry long over wine,
  those who go to try mixed wine.

This is immediately followed by an admonitory maxim:

Do not look at wine when it is red,
  when it sparkles in the cup ...

The four basic functions of wisdom (establishing facts, ordering, admonishing, questioning) belong inseparably together. Aphorisms with the first function state facts that can be confirmed again and again; in this way elements are created for an order of life and a world order which is certainly not unalterably rigid, nor without inner contradictions, but is constantly subjected to new possibilities of confirmation. The exhortations have the function of inaugurating men into the recognized order, the reasons given repeatedly appealing to a perception of the rules of life as these are established in proverbial wisdom. The riddle, finally, asks about the content of knowledge; it has hardly survived in the wisdom literature of the Old Testament, but on the basis of I Kings 10.1ff. we can probably assume that it played an important role in the didactic procedure that went to form wisdom.

The basic presupposition from which wisdom thinking argues is that a man's behaviour and his fate belong inseparably together:

the man who fits into the world order will be upheld by it, the man who behaves well will do well – and vice versa. This axiom – a matter of course for ancient man – is no problem at all for earlier wisdom; it is quite late before it becomes the object of attack.

The upholders of wisdom in ancient Israel: Israelite and non-Israelite wisdom

Many Mesopotamian and Egyptian texts have survived which can be compared with the Old Testament wisdom texts. These make it clear that the *school* must be viewed as the upholder of Mesopotamian and Egyptian wisdom. The main purpose of the schools was to train officials for the administration. The children learnt reading and writing – and learnt them from wisdom texts. The education offered by these schools was highly comprehensive. Popular wisdom (proverbs) was collected here, but in addition there were subjects designed to meet the specific educational requirements of these upper-class children, who were later to enter the administrative service. Thus, for example, the Egyptian teachings are designed to be a guide to proper behaviour in polite society, in the presence of the king, etc.; here a seemly silence, modest behaviour, respect towards superiors, as well as generous and just behaviour towards inferiors, is again and again the subject of exhortation.

There can be no doubt that there were schools of this kind in Israel as well, although oddly enough the Old Testament hardly says anything about them. But the wise man's position ought probably to be connected with institutions of this kind. After Israel, as a state, came to require an administration as finely differentiated as that of other oriental empires, scribal schools were no doubt necessary. Moreover, such schools probably existed not only in the capital (or in the main cities) but in other fair-sized towns as well.

Did Israel *only* know the wisdom of the schools, or must we assume the existence of a more popular wisdom besides – wisdom which would have had its origin, not in the milieu of court and city, but in the sphere of the ancient Israelite clan?

Along these lines, H. W. Wolff speaks of a *clan wisdom*; he tries to show that Amos, the farmer from Judah, bore the stamp of an education in this clan wisdom, and not the wisdom of the court.

It is true that we have to reckon with the fact that 'wisdom' in the ancient East was not bound to the phenomenon of the school, with its essential connection between wisdom and writing. In Israel the 'wisdom of all people of the east' was particularly famed (I Kings 4.30) – and here the reference is to the nomadic peoples west of the desert of Syria and North-west Arabia. Edom was famous for its wisdom as well, although it was certainly not a centre of urban culture (Obad. 8; Jer. 49.7).

Many proverbs, and whole collections of proverbs in the Old Testament, do actually paint the ideal picture of a civil servant – others, on the other hand, rather reflect peasant life. Given that Israelite wisdom absorbs popular insights and rules – proverbs and apodictic commandments – it will be clear that no hard and fast line can be drawn between the wisdom of the clans and the wisdom of the schools. Certainly, wisdom found an excellent and well-defined character in the institution of the school; and this was without doubt true for Israel as well. But strivings towards wisdom will have existed elsewhere also. Whether Amos can be claimed as an exponent of this 'clan wisdom' may be left undecided.

One further striking fact is worth noting. Among Israel's neighbours *nature wisdom* plays an important role. In Mesopotamia above all, lists were made, classifying and cataloguing the features of nature. Similar phenomena were grouped together and their names were set side by side. In this way an attempt was made to grasp the reality of nature in its whole breadth and to master it in words. Similar lists are known from Egypt as well, even though they probably did not play nearly the role there that they did in Mesopotamia.

Now we must also assume the existence of 'list' science of this kind in the early Israelite period as well; at least, Solomon's wisdom in this respect is described (I Kings 5.9ff.). In the extant wisdom literature of the Old Testament, nature wisdom is almost completely lacking; apparently it was little cultivated in Israel. Israel's striving towards wisdom was confined to the human order; nature came to lie outside her range of vision. (Exceptions are to be found e.g. in Job 28; 38ff. Attempts at nature wisdom probably lie behind Gen. 1 as well.)

6. Genres of Prophecy

The prophets first passed on their message by word of mouth, in characteristic situations and with a characteristic intention. Form criticism can therefore be used for the investigations of their discourses in the same way that it is applied to e.g. the saga. Moreover, it is clear from the outset that the prophets use striking freedom in handling the elements of the genre.

In dealing with prophetic modes of speech, research into genres first takes its bearing from earlier prophecy. From this it gathers the linguistic characteristics of the genres and the intentions behind them. In later times these characteristics are no longer so clearly evident among the prophets.

The diatribe (reproach) and the threat

Terminology. Various expressions are in use to describe the same phenomenon; generally, however, the terms 'diatribe' (reproach) and 'threat' are preferred. Westermann stresses the connection of this form of speech with judicial proceedings and hence talks about accusation and judgment. Koch quite rightly pleads for as neutral a terminology as possible – one which does not interpret the facts from the outset. Consequently he calls the two parts of the 'prophecy of disaster' the 'indication of the situation' and the 'prediction'.

The function of the diatribe and the threat (which we generally find linked antiphonally with one another, and which are therefore to be judged as having originally been a single unit) may be explained from two examples:

'Then the word of Yahweh came to Elijah the Tishbite, saying "Arise, go down to meet Ahab king of Israel, who is in Samaria . . . and you shall say to him, 'Thus says Yahweh: "Have you killed, and also taken possession?" Therefore thus (emend.) says Yahweh: "In the place where dogs licked up the blood of Naboth shall dogs lick your own blood!" ' ' (I Kings 21.17-19).

The saying is directed against *an individual*: against King Ahab, who has had Naboth killed in order to gain possession of his land. This injustice is mentioned first of all; then the consequence of the behaviour follows, the word *lākēn*, 'therefore', forming a link between the two. The injustice practised by Ahab will recoil on him; the same destiny will be meted out to him as he has inflicted on the other.

'Proclaim to the strongholds in Ashdod (Assyria)
  and to the strongholds in the land of Egypt,
and say, "Assemble yourselves upon the mountains of Samaria,
  and see the measureless terror within her
  and the oppressed in her midst!"
They do not know how to do right,
  those who store up violence and oppression in their strongholds.
Therefore thus says Yahweh:
  "An adversary shall surround the land;
  he shall tear down your defences from you,
  and your houses shall be plundered" ' (Amos 3.9-11).

The saying is directed against the *people*. Again, the prophet first speaks of the guilt of the part addressed – Samaria (here the prophet calls on the foreign countries who are not involved, as witnesses, using a particular genre, the herald's instruction): then *lākēn* follows, and the 'messenger formula' (see below); the section ends with a prediction of disaster.

In both cases the close connection between diatribe and threat is evident; the former gives the reason for the latter. In the first instance, where the saying is directed against an individual, the reason is a quite concrete one – a particular murder; in the second case, there is more general talk about injustice. This is connected with the fact that the whole people or the whole city is addressed in summary terms. Whereas the saying addressed to the individual is already known in pre-classical prophecy, the earliest known sayings directed against the people as a whole come from Amos. The connection between diatribe and threat displayed here is typical. Often the threat closes with a summarizing observation which again directs attention to the centre of the entire linguistic unit (e.g. Micah 3.1-4; Koch, *concluding characterization*).

In both examples the formula *kōh 'āmar yhwh* is conspicuous. It is termed the *messenger formula*, since it serves to introduce the exact passing on of a message – and not only in connection with the prophets. The messenger uses this formula and then repeats what his lord has charged him to say (cf. e.g. Gen. 32.3ff.).

As in both the examples above, the messenger formula is found especially often between diatribe and threat. From this it would seem to follow that the two genres are not of equal weight, and that the actual Yahweh saying is only to be found in the prediction of disaster; we should accordingly have to see the proof of guilt as being the word of the prophet. At the same time it should be remembered that the messenger formula is also often missing between diatribe and threat, and occasionally it is even placed in front of the diatribe (this is frequently the case in later prophecy). In the first of the two examples mentioned it actually occurs twice, introducing both diatribe and threat.

In a number of prophetic sayings it is impossible to decide exactly whether we are dealing with a threat or with a diatribe. Chief among these doubtful cases are the cries of *hōy* (e.g. Isa. 5.8-24; 10.1-4, a connected sequence of cries of 'woe'). Generally the transition from proof of guilt to prediction of disaster is lacking in these cries. The threatened disaster is already contained in the cry itself, whereas in the description of the injustice, the disastrous consequence is implied.

The origin of the cries of *hōy* – which must not be confused with those formulated with *'ōy* – is disputed. In some places *hōy* is an independent interjection (woe! ha!); otherwise it is generally linked with participles or substantives, giving the reason for the cry. There is clear evidence for the cry *hōy* in the lament for the dead (e.g. I Kings 13.30; Amos 5.16). Whether the cry was known in wisdom formulations as well is open to question.

It at least follows from all that we have said that the offence committed and the disaster predicted are to be viewed in close connection with one another. Again, this is particularly clear in I Kings 21.17ff. The 'culprit' is a victim of his own injustice. Here the connection between act and consequence comes into force (cf. pp. 8of.). Because the prophet calls the injustice by its proper name, it acquires the power of producing disaster. It is true that this connection between act and consequence is strictly viewed as subject to Yahweh's will: the coming disaster is Yahweh's act – hence the frequency of the messenger formula before the prediction of disaster.

Isolated diatribes standing by themselves already imply the prediction of disaster, and predictions of disaster presuppose the guilt that causes them.

It seems that the prophets directed their pronouncements of disaster quite spontaneously against members of their own people (or against the nation as a whole); at least it is nowhere clearly suggested that they were approached for such sayings. Apparently, however, a development took place in the sense that the sayings of disaster were first directed only at individuals (cf. early on the way in which Nathan appears before David in I Sam. 12) and related to specific misdemeanours. Later, they were expanded and made more general, in terms both of the people addressed and their guilt. As a rule the prophets of the eighth century turn to the nation as a whole, reproaching it with disobedience towards Yahweh in a ruthless way which was unknown before that time.

Prophecies of salvation (promises)

(a) Prophecies of salvation to individuals and to Israel. Promises of salvation made to individuals and to Israel are much more rarely represented in pre-exilic written prophecy than prophecies of disaster. Consequently the formal elements are less clearly recognizable.

The prophecy of salvation to individuals can no doubt be traced back to seers and fortune-tellers, who constituted one of the roots of the Israelite prophetic movement. In obscure situations in life, one could make contact with a 'man of God' of this kind in order to acquire insight and guidance for one's behaviour. These men of God often had to prove their soothsaying authority through a 'sign', an easily controllable test of their extraordinary knowledge or ability. Similar figures are also familiar elsewhere in the East, in circumstances which resemble Israel's culturally.

It seems that in Israel prophets of this kind often came forward quite spontaneously in order to approach a man with some prophecy or other – prophecies of salvation or disaster made to the individual will have had their origin here. At all events, the prophecy of disaster to the whole people is to be viewed as a further development of the prophecies of disaster to the individual. Koch thinks that he can discover the same pattern in the prophecies of salvation to the individual as in the prophecies of disaster: indication of situation – prediction of salvation – concluding characterization (e.g. Jer. 28. 2-4; 34.4f.). The evidence which could date from the period of pre-classical prophecy (e.g. I Kings 11.31; 17.14) seems to be extant in a later stylization, so we cannot exclude the possibility that the genre of the prophecy of disaster also had an influence on the prophecy of salvation.

The prophecies of salvation made by the official cultic prophets were also moulded according to a particular genre. Proof of this may be found in the polemic against these prophets with their characteristic cry of *šālōm*, polemic which can be found among the individual prophets, whose proclamation came to set the tone of the course of the Old Testament tradition (cf. pp. 66f.).

These individual prophets mainly proclaim disaster (the authenticity of the few sayings which prophesy salvation alone is highly disputed, e.g. Isa. 2.2ff.: 9.1ff.). At the same time, in Isaiah and Hosea it is suggested that Yahweh's calamitous acts could turn again to good; the idea is then carried forward beyond judgment into an era in which God's order of salvation could once more prevail (Isa. 1.21-26; 7.1-17; Hos. 2.2-15; 14.2-9).

With the exile, the situation altered. Now prophets of salvation appeared whose voices permeate the whole of the Old Testament tradition. (It is from this period, too, that a prophecy of salvation has been preserved which takes up the cry of *šālōm* from the pre-exilic prophecy of salvation, Isa. 57.19.) Deutero-Isaiah was the most influential. He borrowed obviously cultic genres, especially the individual oracle of salvation, using them as a model for a wider proclamation of salvation, which absorbs elements of the communal lament and gives them a positive direction.

The function of these prophecies of salvation is characteristic. They are set in a situation in which Israel really no longer exists as a nation; all the ordinances of salvation have broken down. The prophecies of salvation announce a future in which salvation will break in with that overwhelming force which at present brings only disaster. Both the present experience of disaster (disaster which the people will endure and see through to the end with Yahweh's help) and the expectation of salvation take on dimensions hitherto unknown in Israel (see also pp. 120f.). That is why the linguistic forms which develop at this time are quite new, even when they derive from the cult. The salvation that is proclaimed transcends all previous experience. The same is true of the descriptions of salvation in the post-exilic period, which follow on the proclamation of Deutero-Isaiah (they are to be found above all in Trito-Isaiah, Isa. 56-66, and in the Isaiah apocalypse, Isa. 24-27). A corresponding development can also be shown in the sayings addressed to foreign peoples in post-exilic times.

(b) Prophecies of disaster directed against foreign peoples. Predictions of disaster directed against Israel's enemies – from every possible quarter – are implicitly predictions of salvation for Israel: once the enemy is destroyed, Israel will triumph. A great number of these predictions addressed to Israel's enemies are extant in the Old Testament. As an example we may take Isa. 14.24f.:

Yahweh of hosts has sworn:
'As I have planned,
so shall it be,
and as I have purposed,
so it shall stand,
that I will break the Assyrian in my land,
and upon my mountains trample him under foot.'

The Assyrians have invaded the country, and it is against them that Yahweh's saying is directed; he announces that he will intervene against the enemy.

Unlike predictions of disaster addressed to the prophet's own nation, here a reason is hardly ever given. Nor is it necessary. Israel's enemies are naturally taken to be Yahweh's enemies, a concept for which there is evidence throughout the cultic literature: the hymns praise Yahweh as the one who conquers the enemy and thereby achieves Israel's salvation.

It is probable that these sayings, with ideas which are so closely related to the cult, are themselves from a cultic setting. In this case we would be dealing with *cultic prophecy* as a genre, which of course does not exclude the possibility that the genre was also used here and there by prophets who were not cultic officials.

It is striking that reasons are given in the sayings addressed to the nations in Amos 1f. (1.3-8, 13-15; 2.1-3, 6-9, 12-16) are authentic. What is of prime importance here is the combination of predictions of disaster directed both against the surrounding nations *and* against Israel. The cause of sayings is emphasized most strongly in the prophecy against Israel – but it is then also transferred to the prophecy against the nations. Apparently Amos makes use of the prophecy against foreign nations (which was quite familiar to his hearers) as the prelude to his real concern – the prediction of disaster to Israel. He applies the same standard to the surrounding nations as to Israel, by naming the reason in each case. This shatters the original framework of the prophecies against foreign nations – an example of the way in which the usual verbal intention of a genre is altered in prophecy.

Borrowed genres

In order to pass on their message, the prophets very often use genres which actually derive from quite different spheres of life. Thus Isa. 5.1ff. begins in the form of a love song – only to end with the shrill dissonance of a prophecy of disaster. The contrast gives his words a particularly sinister effect. Amos 5.1f. clothes the prediction of disaster in the form of a dirge; here the alien genre is used to underline the content of the prediction. Many similar examples might be quoted.

Prophetic experience, speech and action

Gunkel already raised the question how we should view the path leading from prophetic experience (which he described as being by nature ecstatic) to speech formed on the basis of genres. It is, of course, true that the *prophets' own accounts* only tell us about the immediate and individual prophetic experience to a very limited extent – at least in the earlier period. Granted, Isaiah, Jeremiah and Ezekiel certainly describe the visions of their call (Isa. 6; Jer. 1.4ff.; Ezek. 1.1ff.). But these descriptions are stamped by typical features; one could speak of a genre of 'visionary description'. The intention is not to give an account of a personal and extraordinary experience but to explain the prophet's mission and legitimation to listeners or disciples. In the description of Amos' visions (Amos 7.1-9; 8.1-3), the prophet's own account of his visionary experience is moulded into a prediction of disaster. Yahweh allows Amos to see visions containing the signs of the impending end. It is true that during the vision the prophet introduces himself, and intercedes for Israel;

but the intersection is in its turn typically prophetic. Some texts make it seem probable that on certain occasions – perhaps on days of national lament – prophets had to assume the office of intercessor for Israel before Yahweh; cf. pp. 66f. The description of the visions therefore gives no insight into the psychological processes which lie behind Amos' prophecies.

A change begins with Jeremiah. The prophetic forms of speech are no longer clearly marked here, and formal language recedes in favour of a more personal speech in which the prophet also brings his personal involvement into play. It is uncertain whether the lamentations passed down in the name of Jeremiah derive from the prophet himself, or whether a later community is here using Jeremiah's fate as an example to demonstrate the way in which a prophet has to struggle with his commission; at all events a picture of the prophet clearly emerges here which depicts him as an individual figure, standing outside the community, who in his solitariness is scarcely capable of coping with the divine charge.

It is important for an understanding of the prophetic sayings to see that action often goes hand in hand with speech; this is described either in the prophet's own account (e.g. Ezek. 4f.) or in an account by an outsider (e.g. Isa. 20). The prophet has to present the content of his message through his behaviour. These *symbolic actions* are certainly more than didactic clarification. Through word and action what is proclaimed begins to be realized: the prophets' appearance is characterized by power; it cannot remain without effect (cf. for example Isa. 9.8; Jer. 23.29). In this connection, it is always stressed that Yahweh remains lord of the events that are predicted and brought about by the prophet; they are not automatic and incapable of correction. We must bear this in mind if we are to avoid misunderstanding the unqualified prediction of disaster of a prophet like Amos.

The question of the relationship between the human word and the Word of God in prophetic preaching has often been discussed. Where the connection between proof of guilt and prediction of disaster is concerned, the problem seems to be relatively clear: the messenger formula generally precedes the prediction of disaster, so that it is in the latter that we should have to see the real word of God, Yahweh's direct revelation. To put it more cautiously: the prediction of disaster reflects the direct knowledge which God has communicated to the prophet. Elements in accounts of the prophetic call and in descriptions of visions support this view; according to these, the prophets of disaster are really only commissioned by Yahweh to announce the disaster and to set it afoot. By contrast, the reason given for the coming disaster (in the 'motive clause') would have to be considered as the achievement of the prophet's own interpretation and his own human thought. This view is supported by the fact that the total disaster predicted often goes beyond what might be expected as the consequence of the actual guilt proved. On the other hand, however, we should remember that often the only thing that happens between the proof of guilt and the prediction of disaster is a demonstration of cause and effect, what one does and what happens to one. Basic knowledge of the coming total disaster and the incongruity between individual proof of guilt and the relevant predictions could be viewed as the precipitation of a long experience of accumulated guilt. The accounts of the prophetic call and the visionary descriptions doubtless do not mark the beginning of the prophetic activity; they are the outcome of prophetic activity over a long period. The central questions which arise in this whole complex of problems are: from where do the prophets draw their knowledge of the future? Is it derived from a special revelatory experience, or does it also issue from experience of the world? Does the prophetic claim to pass on the Word of God arise from processes of experience and behaviour which can be imitated elsewhere, or are we dealing with events exclusive to them? The question of the relationship between theological and psychological modes of interpretation also plays an underlying part here.

III

The Cult and its Content

1. The Background

After the First World War, interest in Israel's cult moved in widely differing ways into the centre of exegetical studies. This was primarily due to the new questions that had opened up within theology generally. Consequently we must first give a brief account of the new approaches in systematic theology during this period.

Form criticism and dialectical theology

In the German-speaking world form criticism underwent a curious development. It is significant that this approach was adopted by New Testament scholars (above all K. L. Schmidt, Martin Dibelius and Rudolf Bultmann). By a process of analogy, Gunkel's insights were first of all utilized for the synoptic gospels; New Testament scholars enquired into the original linguistic units, discovered the oral character of the gospel tradition, searched for the 'setting in life' of the individual fragments, and so on.

New Testament form criticism soon came under the influence of dialectical theology, which made a widespread impact after the First World War. The *sociological* aspect of form criticism now acquired *theological* value in the question about the *Sitz im Leben*. The community plays an important part; it impresses its character on each unit (pericope), and governs the latter's purpose. Now scholars began to enquire more particularly and with direct theological interest into the community and its message. This reflected the concern of the time, to view theology as a function of the church and not as a function of civilization (or culture). Psychological and sociological aspects recede into the background: the statements of the Old and New Testament community are no longer primarily viewed as human utterances, with psychological backgrounds in need of illumination; they are now seen as *kerygma*, as the message of God, which demands obedience rather than sympathetic understanding.

The intentions of dialectical theology are still noticeable in many ways. Here the confrontation between God and man is stressed, and with it the confrontation between the Word of God and the human word. The Word of God is a force which confronts man as an alien power, unmasking the world and natural man in their folly; in this way it is the efficacious word of judgment over everything that belongs to the natural man. The biblical message of the Old and New Testaments is now interpreted in this sense; the message of Christ which it contains means the crisis of all human actions and words.

This also determines the attitude of these scholars to the phenomena of religion: religion is in a quite particular degree subject to the divine judgment. For in religion man attempts to find a way to God, and it is here that human wrong-headedness and self-sufficiency are manifested most clearly of all. 'Christian faith' – i.e. obedience to the Word of God – and religion become opposing terms.

The question put by the history of religions school, which had tried to determine the relationship between the religions of the world and Christianity as the absolute religion, were in this way rejected as illegitimate; and form criticism, conceived by Gunkel in the context of the same comprehensive group of problems, now lent support to a theological approach of a very different kind.

Hence new points of view emerged for the systematic placing of the Old Testament. How is the relationship between the message about Christ and the Old Testament message to be conceived? Does the Old Testament belong on the side of the religions? Is it therefore also subject to judgment, forming the negative foil to the Christ event, to which the New Testament testifies? While recourse to the Lutheran theology of the Reformation raised problems, the twin concepts of law and gospel offered themselves as an explanation of the relationship between the two Testaments.

The other possibility was to move the Old Testament to the side of the message of Christ and to seek 'the witness of the Old Testament to Christ' (the title of a much discussed book by W. Vischer which came out in the 1930s). In different cases this enquiry was carried on in different ways; but the systematic presupposition underlying all the attempts was that there is a historical coherence between the events of the Old and New Testaments which is essentially without parallel in other historical events (Karl Barth talks about the 'primal history'). This, however, means that it is in principle impossible to compare Old Testament faith with the religions of the Ancient East – a premise which the historian is bound to view with scepticism. None the less, in the light of these data it is clear why, under the influence of dialectical theology, form-critical studies were energetically pursued, whereas comparable work in the field of the history of religion receded well into the background.

The theology of religion

Besides dialectical theology we must mention another theological movement, comparable with dialectical theology in many respects and yet tending in a totally different direction. The main impulse was given to it by Rudolf Otto's book, *The Idea of the Holy*, which appeared in 1917 and was translated into English in 1923. Otto, too, speaks of the 'wholly other' which is completely opposed to human rationality; but by this he means the religion whose basic category he describes as 'the holy': it is the *numinosum*, the supernatural-divine, which touches man in religious experience; it is the *mysterium tremendum*, something alien to man, which makes him fear; and the *fascinosum*, that which fascinates him and draws him into its orbit.

The holy is a basic category not only in the history of religion but also in theology; here Christianity appears together with the other religions. Now, religion demands 'cultivation' of the holy, 'cult' (the word comes from the Latin *colere*). Thus in this theological movement the question of worship, the cult, in which the holy manifests itself, is given pre-eminent attention. Again, the function of Christian and non-Christian worship is seen as being the same in principle.

The study of comparative religion has also shown that in all religions there are certain fixed basic forms and 'phenomena' which constantly recur, even though they can differ greatly in intention and content within the unified whole, the 'structure', which constitutes the individual religion. The 'elements' out of which the cult is built also display certain regularities. It is possible to construct a scheme, a 'pattern' for worship, a 'phenomenology' of the cult, the form of which, at least, fits all religions from the lowest up to Christianity (S. Mowinckel, *Religion und Cultus*, p. 9).

Religion is a universal human experience; the holy manifests itself again and again, even if in constantly different forms. And the theological conclusion is:

'The origin of religion is the "revelation" which took place in "creation" ... in all religions there lies a more or less clear spark of true knowledge of the divine' (Mowinckel, op. cit., p. 135).

This theological concern crystallized in various activities. First of all a lively interest arose in the churches, which was especially directed towards the renewal and deepening of the forms of worship. Then the ecumenical movement found its keenest support in these circles: the guiding idea was concentration, not on denominational and theological pecularities, but on the common elements of religious life in the different Christian groups. Finally, attempts were even made to take up the dialogue with other religions, outside the borders of Christianity.

The combination of all these tendencies can easily be exemplified from the activities of prominent theologians. Rudolf Otto concerned himself actively with the movement for liturgical renewal in the 1920s and 1930s; in addition, he founded the 'Religious League of Mankind', in which members of the most widely differing religions were to come together to reflect about the values which they had in common. Nathan Söderblom, a Swedish historian of religions, later Archbishop of Uppsala, was one of the most active promoters of the ecumenical idea; he too played a leading part in the renewal of the forms of worship in his church, writing hymns, etc. A similar proliferation of activities can be found in many other theologians with similar theological interests.

Both dialectical theology and the 'theology of religion' (as we might perhaps briefly call it) were concerned with the confrontation between God and man. But dispute flared up mainly over the phenomenon of religion. Is religion to be assigned to God, as the medium of his revelation? Or is it the quintessence of the world in its perversion?

Trends in the development of Old Testament research

Since the 1920s, different questions in different geographical areas have given Old Testament research their individual stamp. Whereas in Germany exegetical work was mainly influenced by the problems indicated in the opening section of this chapter, Scandinavian and English scholars generally worked against the background of a 'theology of religion'. This was extremely noticeable in the themes of exegetical studies, in their method and their hypotheses. Hence work stemming from the spheres of influence of different 'schools' should always be read carefully against the background of its situation in the history of research.

At the same time, the concept 'school' must be used cautiously. The individual positions of Scandinavian, as well as German, scholars are so differentiated that they cannot simply be lumped together and stamped with a particular label. A man only talks about a 'school' if he does not belong to it himself – and this applies equally to the 'cultic history school', to the 'Bultmann school', and to all the others. Even if a group of scholars shares certain theological presuppositions, and is actuated by the same questions, the crystallization of these concerns in their exegetical work takes place in very different ways.

2. Israel's Cult and the Cults of the Ancient East

The essential impulses of the 'cultic history' approach to the Old Testament go back to Sigmund Mowinckel (1884-1965). His studies of the Psalms (in six volumes, 1921-24) broke new ground in Scandinavia. A movement with a similar trend arose independently in England, first coming to the fore with a collection of studies edited by S. H. Hooke, *Myth and Ritual* (1933).

The function of the cult

It is common to both the scholarly trends we have mentioned that a comprehensive meaning is ascribed to cultic ceremonies: in the cult man and God meet; here man receives life, in the most comprehensive sense. It is from the cult that the real forces spring which order healthfully the life of man – and beyond that the life of nature: blessing, fertility, peace, happiness and health.

The experience of these healthful forces is closely connected with the experience of nature: it is there that blessing, fertility and the rest manifest themselves. But in addition, man also sees sinister forces at work in nature: drought, misfortune and decay. Thus nature is experienced as the dramatic clash of contrasting forces. Moreover, it appears that these forces are embedded in the revolving seasons; drought has its season, renewed fertility has its season, etc. The dramatic clashes of healthful and sinister forces recur periodically year by year; they have a cyclical character.

These dramatic forces are reflected in the events of the cult; there they are depicted in a sacred play, in the cultic drama, which can take the most varied forms: dance, true mimic representation, contest, etc. Now these cultic happenings would not of course be understood as being the reflection of natural events. On the contrary: the real happening takes place in the cult and its effects then come to maturity in nature. It helps the forces of life to achieve a breakthrough. The cultic actions are accompanied by words, by myth (cf. pp. 54f.). Man sees and hears the fundamental event which forms the basis both of his own life and of the life of the world.

This description of the function of the cult is strongly influenced by the study of cultic phenomena in so-called 'primitive' cultures, i.e., civilizations without writing and with little differentiation. Both in Scandinavia and in England ethnological researches into these civilizations (pursued in Scandinavia by V. Grønbech and in England by Sir James Frazer) exerted an important influence on Old Testament scholars.

The New Year festival and the enthronement of Yahweh

The central cultic event marks a revival of forces beneficial to man within a yearly period. It was a New Year festival. In Babylon, for example, the New Year (*akitu*) festival was in fact *the* central cultic happening in the course of the year.

Mowinckel identified this central cultic event with the ancient Israelite autumn festival, which evidently marked the turn of the year (admittedly, it is never called 'the New Year festival' in the Old Testament, but only the 'year's end festival' and 'the turn of the year festival').

What was the specific content of the Israelite New Year festival? In the second volume of his studies of the psalms, Mowinckel draws particularly on the *enthronement psalms*.

The cry *yhwh mālak*, which is characteristic of these psalms, can be translated 'Yahweh has become king'. This means that the cultic drama has just come to an end; Yahweh has victoriously completed his struggle against his numinous opponents and has established his royal rule. Mowinckel therefore interprets the enthronement psalms (cf. here pp. 67f.) only from this thematic angle, ignoring other aspects connected with the history of the genres. Apart from the 'Yahweh is king' psalms, about twenty other psalms are interpreted as enthronement psalms because Mowinckel considers that their content expresses the content of this festival.

The enthronement of Yahweh is the central event in the Israelite New Year festival; the statements in the Old Testament which have a bearing on it are elements in the enthronement myth. (For Mowinckel, myth is not really the term for a genre; it describes a coherent group of cultic ideas.) In addition, other 'myths' also belong to the Israelite New Year festival: the creation myth; the myth of the fight with the dragon; the war of the gods myth (i.e., a myth which tells of God's struggle with hostile gods); the judgment myth (containing Yahweh's judgment on hostile nations); and finally the exodus myth. According to this view, therefore, the main theological themes of the Psalter (and, what is more, of the Old Testament in general) would be elements in the content of Yahweh's enthronement festival. Israel's religion is really to be understood in the light of this central point. Even the facts of salvation history – e.g. the exodus – are preserved in myth; the myth is historicized, or history is turned into myth. Here Mowinckel finds characteristic differences of content between the New Year's festival in Israel and corresponding festivals among Israel's neighbours.

The cultic pattern

Mowinckel already stressed that some essential features of the Israelite New Year festival are also operative in other ancient eastern religions as well. It was on these common features especially that the work of a number of English scholars was concentrated – work which found expression in the collections of studies edited by S. H. Hooke. In these the general theory was put forward that it is possible to establish a 'myth and ritual pattern' which displays the basic structure of all ancient oriental cults.

The pattern is characterized as follows: in the cultic ceremony the central point is the struggle between the forces of death and life in nature. This finds expression in the *death and resurrection of the god*, who first succumbs to the destructive forces, but then attains to new vital power. The god's death is accompanied by wailing and mourning rites, by cultic weeping, lustration ceremonies, and so forth. The resurrection consists of a *struggle* against the forces inimical to life (ritual combat), the manifestations of chaos. The struggle is ritually depicted and is accompanied by the *creation myth*. The victory means that the cosmic powers conquer, their blessing can become efficacious. The power of fertility is made effective through the sacred marriage (*hieros gamos*) which takes place between the king and a priestess. The conclusion is the *triumphal procession* of the god; he receives the homage and acclamation of gods and men.

Of course this pattern does not emerge equally clearly in all ancient oriental cults; sometimes the one element is given more emphasis, sometimes the other; occasionally one element (or more) can be lacking. Here the cultic pattern theory reckons with a variability similar to that which form criticism expects of the genres. The main emphasis lies on the fact that the function and the intention of the cult remain the same; from this a structural analogy results which can then vary considerably in individual cases. The central standpoint is that the cultic happenings take their bearings from the course of nature; ultimately, the cultic pattern theory holds, they are a 'nature cult' (cf. also p. 102).

One important question has not been settled: how did the pattern come into being? Two opposing answers have been given. According to the first, there is *one* historical origin, one ancient oriental culture in which the pattern came into being; from here it spread by means of cultural borrowings, finally determining all ancient eastern religions. The expounders of the myth and ritual movement do sometimes argue in this direction; originally they were strongly stimulated in their work by Egyptologists, and suspected that the origin of the pattern was in Egypt. The opposing opinion holds that when cultural data are analogous, analogous religious structures (and hence cultic patterns) are to be expected. This opinion too – it derives from ethnological researches such as those carried on by Tylor and Frazer – was upheld by the English scholars associated with Hooke. A newer, impressive attempt to show the pattern not only in the ancient east but also in other cultural areas derives from T. H. Gaster. Here the 'anthropological', non-historical explanation of the pattern is expressly moved into the foreground.

The divine kingship

The figure of the king generally plays an important role in researches into the cultic pattern; scholars frequently speak of a 'sacral' or 'divine' kingship. They mean by this that the king himself represents the deity in the celebrations of the cult. When, for example, the suffering and death of the god is cultically realized, it is supposed to have been depicted through the king (or at least through a substitute king); the triumphal procession of the god is again thought to have been realized through the king; and finally it is clear that, according to a number of rituals, the king has to carry out the sacred marriage.

According to this it would be quite clear that the role of the king is the seam-line joining the world of the gods and the world of men: the king actually incorporates the god, he mediates the sacred forces to the world, thereby ultimately uniting in himself the functions of both priest and ruler.

It is important to stress here that the spectrum of variation in the elements of the pattern is a broad one. The 'divinity' of the king is brought out to a varying degree at different times and in different geographical areas. One can most readily talk about a 'divine kingship' in Egypt; here the institution of the monarchy really did have a divine quality. In the Sumerian area the development goes almost as far at a particular period (Ur III), the king appearing as the guardian deity of his country;

all the same, he is not the incarnation of the highest gods; he is merely viewed as their son. The Babylonians and Assyrians avoided the identification between king and god, though it is always stressed that the monarchy is instituted by the gods. This indeed is a basic feature of all views of kingship in the ancient east: the office of king is created and instituted by the gods; the king has to represent the will of the gods and to enforce it against all the forces inimical to life, both within the country and outside it. He is therefore the god's representative. How far divine attributes were assigned to this office varies; the distance between the divine and the human differed considerably.

Nature and history

In research into the history of the cult, the natural basis of every cultic ceremony was emphatically stressed. However, it was not sufficiently noticed that history, politics and law also play an essential part in the cults of the Ancient East. That is already shown by a superficial glance through the cultic literature drawn from all the spheres of Israel's environment, from Sumeria to Egypt. According to statements in the Mesopotamian hymns, for example, the function of the king as the representative of the deity comprises more than the promotion of fertility (though this played an important part); he also had to wage war against the country's enemies and thus to protect the state against the outside world, indeed ever to enforce a claim to universal rule. In addition he had to see that justice and peace were established internally, to punish evil-doers and to root out injustice; finally, in the wisdom that belonged to him as king he had to see to it that all the different things which make up a country's prosperity – cult, war, justice – found their proper fulfilment. In all the spheres of life we have mentioned we really have to do with aspects of a single comprehensive order, which embraces the whole of life in its natural and cultural totality.

The events of the cult assume this all-embracing order – and not merely the order of nature. Thus the myth, too, is not unrelated to the historical and political experience of a people; in many myths it is possible to show that historical events have found their literary expression in certain features of mythical narrative. And when, for example, the Babylonian New Year myth of *enuma elish* has a struggle as its centre, we should probably think less of the forces of nature inimical to life which have to be banished, than of forces in the political sphere. The victory over the enemy gods in the myth introduces the victory over enemy nations.

We meet a curious kind of historical thinking here. History is not seen as a linear development, and the historical law of the unique event has no validity. History is rescinded in a world order which finds expression in a cyclical rhythm and which is given archetypal validity.

For in the earlier of the advanced civilizations, historiography is not a report about what happened. This function is fulfilled by mythical narrative ... History finds existence as it has come to be, already present; at its beginning stands the permanent form which the world reached in the era of creation. Thus history becomes cult, which upholds this being, whose order is given by the creator; it becomes a feast which continually renews and realizes the mythical happenings of the prim-aeval period. Concepts like progress and development have no place in this non-linear view of history; for according to this view, the world belongs within the movement of history in the same way that it belongs within the movement of the constellations, which run their course according to fixed laws yet without goal and end (E. Hornung, *Geschichte als Fest*, pp. 46f.).

Cultic phenomenology and cultic history

The different outlines of the cultic patterns in the religions of the Ancient East are marked by a common procedure: the various cults are described or reconstructed (detailed ritual information is only at our disposal in a few cases), are compared with one another, and are interpreted in the light of their common ground. At no point, therefore, can we actually lay hold of the 'basic pattern' of the cult itself; in fact we only meet the pattern in concrete terms in its different variations.

This procedure is not without its dangers. Differences in the individual religions are often levelled out. It can easily happen that a particular cultic element is wrongly interpreted, when it is interpreted from the outside – i.e., in the light of similar data in other cults.

It is obvious that a cultic element must first be viewed in its

historical context. The directly related historical circumstances offer
the most probable explanation for the elucidation of a phenomenon.
Generally these related circumstances are not, it is true, immediately
evident; they can only be inferred. Historical reconstructions of
this kind are continually necessary; and here one must always
explain the reasons in favour of, or against, the reconstruction and
point out where the uncertain factors lie; in this way it will also be
possible to assess the degree of probability.

The descriptive work of phenomenological observation can only
provide the framework for studies in the field of religious history.
Its importance must not of course be underestimated. The working
out of patterns in the cult by phenomenological methods first of
all creates a field of concepts, meanings and ideas of which the
historian of religion can make use; this field will be better fitted
to its subject than the unconsidered use of a terminology which
springs from modern Western European feeling. 'Cultic phenomenology' and 'cultic history' must not therefore be played off
against one another, as is frequently the case in Old Testament
exegesis.

Under these aspects, the relation of Israelite religion to other ancient
oriental religions can be adequately described – e.g. in terms of its
'cultic pattern'. When the perspectives of both cultic phenomenology
and cultic history are given their due weight, the fact emerges that
Israel's religious thinking and behaviour is on the one hand closely
bound up with its environment, yet on the other displays its own quite
specific expressions and developments of cultic phenomena – like all
the other ancient oriental cults. It is as perverse to contrast Israel and
all the other religions of the ancient east as it is to smooth down all
historical differences in favour of a cultic pattern or to reject the history
of religion or phenomenology altogether.

3. The Special Position of Israel's Cult

It is clear that the scholarly trend described above, which stressed
the features common to the Israelite cult and the cults of other
ancient oriental countries, takes its bearings from Israel at the
period of the monarchy. In Germany, where people were much

more interested in the unparallelled peculiarities of Israelite religion, attention focussed increasingly on Israel's early period, on the settlement in Palestine and the growth of the nation before the monarchy. It was here that scholars hoped to find the features which gave Israel's faith its special stamp. In concrete terms, the questions were: how was Israel constituted before the monarchy? What form did its worship take? And in what way did Yahweh appear in that worship?

Martin Noth's amphictyonic theory

Martin Noth's book *Das System der zwölf Stämme Israels* appeared in 1930, and its theory made an immense impact on the German-speaking world. Noth starts from the observation that lists of twelve Israelite tribes appear in several places in the Old Testament. There are some differences in the make-up of these tribal lists, but the number – twelve – is constitutive. Some of the tribes mentioned are known almost solely from lists of this kind. For example, Reuben, Simeon and Levi apparently no longer played any part at all in the period immediately preceding the constitution of the nation – they were no longer in existence at all as tribes; they had dissolved, their sub-divisions being absorbed into other Israelite tribes. On the other hand, groups are mentioned here and there in the Old Testament which are not to be found in any tribal list.

This fact already suggested to Noth certain important conclusions: the list of tribes, for which the number twelve is constitutive, at least derives from the period before Israel became a nation, since afterwards the tribal organization played no further role. Some of the tribes had disappeared completely from the scene and political conditions at the time of the monarchy simply do not fit the tribal lists at all. But these lists do not give any information about any political arrangements in an earlier period either, because apparently at the time when some tribes were constituted in the final phase of the settlement, other tribes (e.g., Reuben) no longer existed as a separate unit any more.

Now Noth points out that it is not only the tribes of Israel that are enumerated in lists of twelve; Nahor's twelve sons (Gen. 22.20ff.)

and Ishmael's twelve sons (Gen. 25.13ff.) are mentioned in a similar way. Apparently these are tribal groups, comparable sociologically with the Israelite tribal alliance. Noth finds the key to an understanding of the function of these associations of twelve (perhaps there were also associations of six – Noth finds indications of this in the Old Testament) in the ancient Greek and Italian institution of the *amphictyony*. These amphictyonies were cultic communities which were formed from a particular number of politically independent units – here too the number twelve, and sometimes six, seems to be constitutive. Those involved in the cult were subject to a common amphictyonic law, which regulated certain affairs connected with the protection and upholding of the common sanctuary. Some cultic acts are performed by the members in common. Beyond this bond of the common cult, there were hardly any links between them; they kept their full political sovereignty.

Noth suspects that institutions of this kind stand behind the lists of twelve (or six) in the Old Testament. For early Israel this would mean that Israel was an association of tribes, whose purpose was not political but rather the upholding of a common cult; the common God is Yahweh; the name of the amphictyony is Israel. (In addition Noth believes that there was an older amphictyony of six, made up of the Leah tribes, whose common God would not yet have been Yahweh.) The central cultic object is the ark, which was moved from place to place (Shechem, Gilgal, Bethel, Shiloh); the tribes are represented by spokesmen (*nᵉśīʾīm* – these also are listed in twelves). An amphictyonic law can also be detected; in later investigations Noth claims that there was an office of 'minor judge', responsible for overseeing the law of the covenant. The law of the covenant is to be found in the oldest parts of the 'Book of the Covenant', particularly where there are apodictic formulations.

The ancient Israelite amphictyony was an institution which could be claimed to have produced the specifically Israelite features of the cult; and it was to these that research in the German-speaking countries gave keen attention.

The amphictyonic hypothesis was largely accepted in Germany for a number of decades; but in recent times critical voices have been increasingly heard. Can the cultural and sociological situation of the Greek and Italian amphictyonies be compared with the tribes and their groups of twelve which are named in the Old Testament? Did the ark really play the part of a central sanctuary for the tribes? Nothing is known of its presence in Shechem (although the first amphictyonic centre is supposed to have been here), and its stationing in Bethel and Gilgal is historically doubtful. The office of minor judge and the functions of the apodictic law are also disputed (cf. pp. 75f. above). Should we not also expect that the amphictyony, if it was *the* central institution in ancient Israel, would also have had a name which could be found in the Old Testament?

The amphictyonic hypothesis is able to explain difficult problems in the early history of Israel – for instance, the fact that although the Israelite tribes did not constitute a political unity before the formation of the nation, they nevertheless viewed themselves as a community and recognized Yahweh as their God. The question is only whether the amphictyonic theory does not raise more problems than it solves. In that case other historical hypotheses would be preferable.

The specific features of the cult in ancient Israel

(a) The tradition of the Sinai covenant according to G. von Rad. For the term 'tradition' see pp. 114f. below. The most important stimuli in the question of the cultic traditions of early Israel came from Gerhard von Rad 'The Problem of the Hexateuch' (1938), in *The Problem of the Hexateuch and other Essays*, 1966, pp. 1ff. Von Rad starts from the following observation about the history of tradition: in many of the biblical confessions, the exodus and the settlement in the promised land appear together, but the events on Sinai are not mentioned. Accordingly, the exodus and the Sinai events do not belong together in the tradition, even though the accounts follow one another in the Book of Exodus; incidentally, this observation can be supported by the findings of literary criticism and transmission history.

Von Rad therefore looked for the cultic roots of the Sinai tradition – he had no doubt that they actually existed:

It is evident that such material does not exist in some nebulous sphere of piety, nor is it the creation of a more or less personal religiosity; it belongs to the official worship, and is in fact fundamental to the worshipping community. Its function therefore is to be sought in the public religious activity of the community, that is to say, in the cultus ...

Mowinckel sees in the narratives of the events at Sinai none other than an account of the New Year Festival, translated into the language of literary mythology. If the constituent materials of the tradition are considered from this point of view, there can be no possible doubt of the fact that they were originally deeply rooted in the cultus ('The Problem', p. 21).

In his evaluation of the function of the cult, therefore, von Rad agrees with Mowinckel; the paths of the two scholars divide at the point where Mowinckel wants to interpret the Sinai myth as an element in the enthronement festival. Von Rad looks for the *original* Sinai festival. He finds clues in two psalms particularly (50 and 81), and in the structure of Deuteronomy; further indications emerge from Josh. 8.3ff.; 24, and from some other passages.

Out of all this von Rad reconstructs the following elements, which he believes marked the course of the festival ritual:

1. Description of the events on Sinai
2. The reading of the law
3. The sealing of the covenant
4. Blessings and curses

The central event is the appearance of God, who declares his will; the people has to commit itself to this will, which finds its expression in commandments; finally, blessings and curses are proclaimed, as the consequences of obedience or disobedience on the part of the Israelites.

The festival took place in autumn; it is identical with the Feast of Tabernacles; its original site was Shechem (cf. Deut. 31.10f.; 27), one of the centres of the amphictyony. Here, accordingly, the tribal association would have solemnized Yahweh's declaration of will in the cult; the feast of the covenant at Shechem seems to be the basis for Israel's understanding of itself as Yahweh's people (cf. p. 72 above).

(b) The tradition of exodus and settlement according to G. von Rad. Von Rad finds a fundamental historical confession of salvation in the 'short historical creed', Deut. 26.5ff. This runs:

A wandering Aramean was my father; and he went down into Egypt and sojourned there, few in number; and there he became a nation, great, mighty, and populous. And the Egyptians treated us harshly, and afflicted us, and laid upon us hard bondage. Then we cried to Yahweh the God of our fathers, and Yahweh heard our voice, and saw our affliction, our toil, and our oppression; and Yahweh brought us out of Egypt with a mighty hand and an outstretched arm, with great terror, with signs and wonders; and he brought us into this place and gave us this land, a land flowing with milk and honey.

A whole series of other texts varies the basic content of the short historical creed; but the basic content is the sojourn in Egypt and the liberation from its oppression in the exodus, together with the bringing of the people into the cultivated land and the conferring of the land of Canaan. The final phase provides the topical reference of the short creed, since it is followed by an indication of the situation: 'And behold, now I bring the first of the fruit of the ground, which thou, O Yahweh, hast given me.'

On the basis of this information, von Rad identifies the feast to which this cultic tradition belongs: it is the Feast of Weeks, which is celebrated at the beginning of the harvest. The original place is thought to have been Gilgal, for almost all the stories of the settlement in the Book of Joshua are concentrated on the tribal area of the Benjaminites and are connected with Gilgal. Here possession and distribution of the land would have played an important historical role. Again, Gilgal is thought to have been an amphictyonic centre, and again the content of the festival was made the common possession of the amphictyony.

(c) Further developments and criticism of von Rad's theory. Von Rad's theories underwent various further developments. For instance, attempts were made to comprehend the cultic ceremonies in Gilgal more clearly; it was conjectured that Josh. 3f. is the literary crystallization of a cultic repetition of the events of the settlement, in which the ark would have played an important part; or an attempt was made to put the election of Israel by Yahweh (who would have been celebrated as the king of his people) at the centre of the festival at Gilgal; the relationship in the cult between the exodus events and the settlement were also discussed. The Passover

was suggested as the date of the festival instead of the Feast of Weeks.

The theory of the 'covenant renewal festival' was also developed further. Some scholars drew on Hittite contract formularies for an explanation: the 'covenant formulary' was thought to correspond to the contract formulary – although here there was no human partner, but a completely unequal relationship between God and Israel. This was taken to explain the differences between the two formularies. A. Weiser finally included both exodus and Sinai tradition in one covenant festival, conceiving the relationship as being one between 'proclamation of being' and 'proclamation of will'.

In all these further developments, which we have only been able to touch on here, one principle remains: the essential features which give the ancient Israelite faith its character have their place in the cult; and this cult is important for the whole amphictyony. This explains the binding nature of the content of their faith for the whole of Israel. Yet this content can go back, in its historical origin, to the experiences of a single tribe or even smaller units of what later came to be Israel. A cultic background is sought for and found for every idea which can be called relevant in Israel's early period. And yet the way in which hypotheses are built up is frequently no less hazardous than it is in Scandinavian and English outlines of cultic history.

Criticism of the theory of a 'covenant festival' and a 'theology of the covenant' has started at the most widely differing points. We have already spoken about the doubtfulness of the existence of an amphict-yony. A precise semantic analysis of the word *berīt* shows that it is inadmissible to talk about a 'covenant' at all. The expression means 'obligation'; in theological use it is applied either to the personal obliga-tion towards Israel assumed by Yahweh, or to an obligation laid on man. The *berīt* theme only acquired greater meaning in the Deuter-onomic and Deuteronomistic eras. Earlier material has obviously been reworked at a later stage in the direction of a *berīt* theology. The short historical creed in its present form is without any doubt extant in a Deuteronomic revision. If one attempts to go back to an older basic form, the parts which tell of the exodus and the settlement in Palestine fall away; there remains an offertory formula, which contrasts the miserable existence of the nomad with the blessings of the tiller of the ground who brings his first fruits in gratitude to Yahweh.

(d) The holy war. In his book *Der Heilige Krieg im alten Israel* (1951), von Rad tried to prove a further element in the amphictyonic cult. 'It is easy to prove that we have to do here with a sacral institution in the fullest sense of the word – if proof is needed at all' (pp. 5f.). 'Proof' here means that a 'theory', the picture of a regular and typical course of a war, is established out of the most varied texts. The following are the characteristic elements of the pattern:

1. The levying of the militia through the blowing of trumpets;
2. Sacrifice and the questioning of Yahweh about the impending struggle;
3. An oracle, with a formula of deliverance ('Yahweh has given the Xs into your hand');
4. Advance to war, with Yahweh at the head of Israel; Israel has to trust in his leadership and his power;
5. The enemy is struck with 'the fear of God' and becomes confused; consequently actual battle is sometimes never joined;
6. Victory is completed with a ban on the enemy; that is to say, all enemy life is annihilated;

(The most complete and concise description is to be found in Judges 4.14-16).

How was this cultic institution realized in history? Here even von Rad sees difficulties. He establishes that the sacred association of the amphictyony did not have sufficient coherence for the realization of this theoretical institution. 'We are therefore dealing here with a cultic institution which never emerged completely in historical terms in its real and intended form' (p. 29). But he attaches all the more importance to the results of this institution; it left behind it in Israel faith in Yahweh's intervention in history, and its effects were felt down to the latest period.

The evidence that the holy war was 'a cultic institution' belonging to 'the sacral tribal league' is very thin. Is it admissible to talk about 'institutions' if they only exist 'theoretically'? At all events, not a single war before the period of the monarchy was carried on by all the tribes; as a rule particular tribes, and occasionally tribal coalitions, were involved. The 'theory' of the regular course taken by a holy war seems much more likely to be a product of the late period, which looked back to those wars and interpreted them as the common past of the tribes. That there were from earliest times Yahwistic wars in the most varied regions of Israel is of course certain; but they were not a cultic institution; rather in each given case, they provided a unique experience of Yahweh's help.

(e) Prophecy and cult. Mowinckel had already expounded the theory that the prophets played an important role in Israel's cult (*Psalmenstudien* III, 1923). For a number of psalms he postulates the function of a cultic prophet, and he makes prophecy above all responsible for the eschatologization of cultic ideas (on the concept of eschatology see p. 124). His ideas found a lasting echo. Here and there attempts were made to prove the existence of cultic prophecy everywhere in the Ancient East, making this phenomenon, too, part of the general cultic institutions through which the pattern was expressed.

Von Rad took up these suggestions and modified them. He gave the cultic prophets their place in the cult of the covenant. They proclaimed Israel's state of salvation, which was guaranteed by the covenant (hence their characteristic cry *šālōm*, cf. pp. 66f. 88 above). One of the special functions of these prophets was intercession, in which they brought Israel's transgressions before Yahweh and tried to win forgiveness. It is therefore possible to speak of a cultic prophecy of salvation.

How, on the other hand, are we to judge the prophecy of disaster? This problem has been discussed especially in the light of the prophet Amos. E. Würthwein pursued the question in two studies (1949/50, 1952). He first of all points out that in Amos the element of intercession appears in the account of a vision. This makes it probable that Amos, too, first belonged to the cultic prophets who proclaimed and effected salvation. But it emerges in the vision that Yahweh is going to bring disaster to Israel; thus Amos becomes the prophet of disaster. He gives a reason for his predictions of disaster, however, and appeals to the norms of justice which are laid down in the law of the covenant; he appeals, that is to say, to the basis of the amphictyony, from whose cult he comes. In the second study

Würthwein even goes a step further. He now suspects that even the prophetic talk of judgment itself has its setting in the cult; we ought to think of a proceeding in which Yahweh (represented by a prophet) appears before the cultic congregation and reproaches it with its transgressions against the amphictyonic law. And in actual fact Yahweh does appear as judge in a number of psalms (e.g., Pss. 96.11-13; 50.1-7).

Würthwein's approach has been developed further, particularly by H. Graf Reventlow. Amos (and other prophets as well) is now seen entirely in the framework of a prophetic office which he thinks had its place in the liturgy of the covenant festival. A fundamental distinction between the prophecy of salvation and the prophecy of disaster is disputed; both are simply an expression of the proclamation of the covenant. According to this view of things, prophecy no longer forms an independent movement; it is only one part of the all-embracing institution of the cult. Amos and men like Amos are no longer judged as *individual* prophets; they are integrated in the cult just as much as any priest.

Criticism of these theories has been both various and energetic. Amos mentions no amphictyony and no covenant; he names neither Sinai nor Moses. It is true that echoes of certain commandments – from the Book of the Covenant, for instance – can be found, but no more. Amos' message consists of a single no: 'no' to the belief in election, 'no' to the cult, 'no' to the people of Israel in general. And that can hardly have been part of the ideas of the cult, however interpreted.

The religion of Yahweh inside the cult and outside it

There is no doubt at all that the Israelite tribes had their cultic customs before Israel became a nation even in their nomadic past. Admittedly no direct evidence of these is extant, and the scholar is therefore dependent on a process of reconstruction.

The theories mentioned on pp. 107ff. are based on two different premises: first, on the amphictyonic hypothesis, which (through comparison with other ancient cultic communities) claims the existence of a cultic-sociological institution. (In the same way, for example, a comparison has been made between 'divine kingship' in Israel and elsewhere in the Ancient East, with the difference, admittedly, that the king of Jerusalem is mentioned in the Old Testament and is in fact sometimes given particular attributes, whereas an 'amphictyony' is never expressly mentioned at all.) The second basic conviction is that the essential religious traditions and ideas – and above all their roots in faith in God's activity in history – were already present in Israel's cult before the monarchy. These convictions explain the tendency (both past and present) to try to trace back the essential elements of Old Testament religion to their roots in the early amphictyonic cult.

We have already spoken briefly about the difficulties with which the amphictyonic hypothesis is burdened. Attempts to reconstruct the cult of Yahweh in the early period are legitimate enough – but they can only produce quite uncertain results because Old Testament information on this point is very sparse; incomparably more criteria are at our disposal for the reconstruction of cultic ceremonies in the period of the monarchy, especially in Jerusalem. Finally, it is hardly true that faith in Yahweh would have ever been expressed exclusively in the cult (i.e., in an institutionalized liturgy performed by particular ministers). For the religion of Yahweh, non-cultic forms of experience and speech played an important part at every period of time (cf. pp. 127ff.).

4. *The Concept of the History of Tradition*

Concern with the celebration of Israel's cult gave rise to increased concern over the methodological aspects of exegetical studies. Scholars not only investigated the forms of cultic proceedings (a question concerned with the history of genres); they also enquired into the content of those proceedings. This was not a random matter. Quite definite themes were passed on in the performance of the cult as well. (The 'main theme' of the Babylonian New Year cult, for example, is the struggle with chaos; it appears in the form of myth, cf. pp. 40ff., 54). The term 'tradition' became a regular term for this material. It is evident, however, that a tradition is determined not only by a 'main theme' but by a whole bundle of ideas and by their stereotyped linguistic expression (i.e., the typical ideas have their own 'word field', a characteristic vocabulary and formulations). 'Traditions' or 'complexes of tradition' are subject to development; so in many cases there is such a thing as a history of the tradition.

Traditions of this kind exist, not only in the cultic sphere, but wherever particular accepted groups of ideas have been arrived at – ideas which are centred on certain theological themes and which present themselves in a consistent linguistic form. Prophecy has also created complexes of tradition, and so to an eminent degree has the Deuteronomic movement. The questions which have crystallized out through a study of the cult have been transferred to other spheres with equal profit.

Other methodological aspects. The terms 'transmission history' (*Überlieferungsgeschichte*) and 'traditional history' (*Traditionsgeschichte*) are sometimes used interchangeably by certain scholars. It is worth making a distinction, because there is a clear difference between the transmission of a single text or a single story (orally or in writing) and the passing on of a particular complex of ideas, which finds expression in different texts. The nomenclature is arbitrary but the use of the terms 'transmission history' (which covers the scope of the oral transmission of a single linguistic block, cf. pp. 51f.) and 'tradition history' has become largely accepted in German scholarship and it is to be hoped that this terminology will become universal.

Traditions can appear in different literary types; there is therefore no direct connection between form criticism and tradition history; the Jerusalem tradition about the struggle with chaos, for example, appears in very different literary forms (see for example Pss. 77.16ff.; 89.9f.; 104.5ff.; Isa. 51.9f.). That certain traditions are more deeply rooted in certain literary forms than in others is certain; thus we may assume that the original home of even this tradition about the struggle with chaos was the genre of myth.

IV

Approaches to the Systematic Treatment
of the Old Testament

Finally, we must discuss the systematic treatment of the Old Testament, considering it under three aspects: first of all we shall look at attempts to interpret Yahweh religion as a whole, from the perspective of the history of religion; then we shall indicate the different spheres of experience in which Israel experienced Yahweh as its God (which will involve a description of some of the elements of Old Testament theology); finally, we shall come to the determination of the relationship between the Old and New Testaments, or between Christ and the Old Testament, which brings us to the question of an evaluation of the Old Testament from the perspective of systematic theology.

1. Elements in the History of Israelite Religion

The roots of Israelite religion and its syncretistic development

It is an established fact of scholarship that Israelite religion developed from a number of different roots which are closely bound up with other ancient oriental religions.

This is true in the first place of Israel's God, Yahweh. In Egyptian lists dating from the thirteenth century BC, the name of Yahweh probably occurs for the first time; there it is mentioned in connection with Bedouins who were in contact with the Egyptians on the frontier. In addition, a different list mentions other Bedouins as occupying a certain strip of land which is probably to be identified with the Old Testament Seir, and therefore belongs within the Edomite area of southern Palestine, east of the Arabah.

This accords with the information given in the Old Testament. Here Yahweh is traditionally associated with Sinai, or the mountain of God; it was known that a divine appearance took place there, a theophany. Yahweh 'comes', 'radiates', 'shines' from the direction of Edom-Seir-Teman-Paran; Sinai must be sought there (the information all points in the same direction). The description of the theophany in Ex. 19 suggests a volcanic phenomenon, and there are geological features which would accord with this in north-west Arabia, east of the Gulf of Aqaba, south of the Edomite area. It is here, therefore, that Sinai may be located with some degree of probability (and not on the present-day Sinai peninsula).

Further indications suggest that the Yahweh of Sinai was not only the God of certain clans which were later absorbed into the Israelite people. In Ex. 18, for example, it is clear that there was some cultic contact with the Midianites; a foreigner who lived near the mountain of God, and who according to some passages had a priestly function, is named as being Moses' father-in-law (the information differs in details). Thus the Midianite or Kenite hypothesis is backed by some degree of probability; this theory holds that Yahweh was originally not only the God of some pre-Israelite clans, but was in the first place the *numen* (dwelling near Sinai) of the Kenites or Midianites, and that a considerable number of nomadic clans may have made pilgrimages to him.

On the other hand, these nomadic groups undoubtedly had their clan religion. In the stories about the patriarchs, we often hear about 'the God of the Father' or 'the God of X'. In Gen. 31.53 we hear about an agreement between two clans, where the God of Abraham and the God of Nahor are appealed to as guarantors. This suggests that every group had its clan deity; it was simply called 'the God of the father', i.e. the *numen* who had been revered by the ancestors of the clan. However, these deities also seem to have had special names; for example, in the passage just mentioned, Gen. 31.53, we find the expression *paḥad yiṣḥaq* ('kinsman' or 'fear of Isaac' – the translation is uncertain). These gods of the fathers go with their clans, see to it that they prosper, and are without any local ties. The tribal forefather in each case counts as the bearer of revelation.

The notion of 'Gods of the fathers' is disputed. Alt, who was the first to investigate this type of religion, saw faith in the 'God of the fathers' as being an essential root of Israel's religion.

'Their (i.e. the Gods of the fathers) association with particular groups of men, families, clans, or tribes, their providential oversight over the fortunes of their worshippers in the desert, and where they had settled, their concern with social and historical events – all this recurs only on a higher level and over a much wider field, in the character of Yahweh as the God of Israel ... the Gods of the fathers were *paidagogi* leading to the greater God, who later replaced them completely' (pp. 60, 62).

V. Maag goes further along the same lines:

'In a tribe of herdsmen, the relationship between God and man necessarily runs its course in an extremely simple framework. Very few cultic rules are followed. Devotion cannot take concrete form in the cult, but only in obedience to inspiration and in trust in the power and goodness of the deity ... Nomadic religion is a religion of promise, for the nomad lives in the world of migration, not in the cycle of seedtime and harvest ... In the realm of transmigration, happening is experienced as a going forward, and as a leaving behind. There, existence is experienced as history. This god leads into a future which is not only a repetition and confirmation of the present, but also the goal of the events that are now taking place. The goal gives meaning to the wanderings and their perils; and today's decision to trust in the God who is invoked is pregnant with significance for the future. That is the nature of promise in the light of transmigration.'

This would mean that the seeds of the most essential features of Israelite religion (historical thinking, eschatology) were already sown in the nomadic religion of the fathers.

Other scholars view such extensive descriptions of the nomadic religion of the fathers with reserve; authentic accounts are, of course, lacking, and the stories of the patriarchs are stamped by the attitudes of a later period. At the same time, clan gods are known to have existed in Israel's environment (here, too, the phrase 'the God of my father' is sometimes used) and inspired men apparently played an important role in the religions of Semitic nomads from time to time; a comparison with ethnological parallels in recent nomadic civilizations may cautiously be drawn upon to illuminate the religion of the fathers. But many questions of detail still have to be cleared up here.

Other phenomena might be mentioned in connection with the

intertwining of the roots of Israel's religion with those of other Semitic nomadic religions; the ark, for instance, the tent of meeting, some of the characteristics of prophecy, some elements in the waging of religious war.

We have already mentioned frequently how much Israel's religion was also rooted in the religion of Canaan, and hence, more generally in the sphere of the ancient religions of the East, which were moulded by a settled culture. Here by far the greatest part of the Israelite cult and Israelite wisdom had its origin, as well as important statements about God and theological themes (Yahweh as king, Yahweh as the lord of fertility and nature, Yahweh as creator of the world, and as the conqueror of the powers of chaos).

Just as the upholders of different religious traditions were united in the people of Israel, so the varied religious elements themselves were also brought into a coherent pattern. Israel's religious history can be viewed as the development of different religious systems and structures in tension. Having evolved from different origins, they came into contact with one another and mutually enriched each other – yet were not simply complementary. Here numerous conflicts had to be survived. In this connection it is especially noticeable that the reaction of Israelite religion towards its Canaanite roots was one of increasing rejection. After Canaanite religious ideas and cultic usages had apparently been adopted by the Israelites to a great extent, certain groups began to view particular religious practices of Canaanite origin as incompatible with Yahweh. This tendency went so far that in the Old Testament, whatever is 'Canaanite' often appears as being idolatry *par excellence* (e.g. in Deuteronomy). On the other hand, important features inherited from Canaanite religion of course remained an undisputed part of Yahweh religion (Yahweh as the lord of nature and fertility, creation, the festal calendar, etc.).

An unimportant but significant example of this development is the fate of one of the cultic objects out of the temple in Jerusalem, the 'brazen serpent' (Nehushtan). This was a cultic object of Canaanite origin; similar images belonged to the normal equipment of the ancient oriental temple; scholars assume that there was some connection with the symbolism of the struggle with chaos. In Num. 21.4-9 this object is associated with the nomadic wanderings in the desert; it appears as an apotropaic remedy against dangerous winged serpents. Moses is said to have made the brazen serpent, and this intergrates the cultic symbol in the treasury of experience of the nomadic Israelites; in this way, harmony between the Canaanite sacred object and nomadic feeling would seem to have been achieved. But according to II Kings 18.4, Nehushtan was removed from the temple – so apparently the synthesis proved after all to be an impossible one for Israelite sensibility.

The influence of individual figures on the history of Israelite religion

Moses is very often named as the founder of Israel's religion, and indeed the Old Testament assigns to him an overwhelming multiplicity of functions and tasks; he appears as mediator between Yahweh and Israel, to whom he has to communicate the divine name; he is the authorized leader of his people in the events of the exodus; he is the lawgiver on Sinai. In this way almost everything which, according to Israelite self-understanding, is important for Yahweh religion is traced back to Moses.

Historical-critical research has come to see that Moses' manifold functions are to a large extent the product of transmission history. Martin Noth arrives at an extremely sceptical judgment with regard to the figure of Moses which the historian claims to recognize; in his opinion, Moses is almost everywhere a latecomer in transmission history, and the only remaining assured historical fact is that he lived, was married to a foreigner, and finally died. Noth finds that the location of Moses' tomb which has been passed down to us has the firmest historical basis; and for this reason he thinks that Moses should probably be given a place in the framework of the events leading up to the settlement.

Most scholars have a more positive view about the possibility of establishing Moses' historical position. It has been pointed out that he has an Egyptian name. This suggests that Moses really was connected with the exodus events. But, since the exodus seems to have been understood from the very beginning entirely as Yahweh's act, it is permissible to view as authentic the link between Yahweh, Moses and the exodus. The historical circumstances which are shown in the book of Exodus can easily be reconciled with what is known from Egyptian sources for the period of Ramesses II (1290-1223 BC). Thus Moses will really have played a decisive role in the flight of his group from Egypt; and it can hardly be doubted that this event was seen as being the act of Yahweh, so that Moses counted as Yahweh's pre-eminent representative and the mediator of his revelation.

It is, of course, uncertain how we ought to characterize Moses' faith. In what form was Moses familiar with the Sinai tradition? Did the prohibition against recognizing other gods exist? Were there other characteristic Yahweh commandments in the religion of Moses? It is useless to speculate about these things. At any rate, Moses' activity and influence released impulses of fundamental significance for Israelite religion; and the development of transmission history makes it quite clear that these impulses contained the trend towards recognizing Yahweh as the only effective God for his worshippers, and the one who made the highest demands on them.

In later times, too, new impulses for the formation of Yahweh religion came from individual figures. We can think of David, who fetched the ark, Israel's sacred symbol, to Jerusalem and there integrated it into the Canaanite cult, a considered act of religious policy which encouraged syncretism. The same tendency is to be seen in the dynasty of Omri in northern Israel. Of course, these kings roused the criticism of intransigent Yahweh worshippers like Elijah, who protested against the co-existence of Yahweh and Baal. At first the proclamation of the great individual prophets faded away unheard – but later it had lasting and far-reaching effects in Deuteronomic and Deuteronomistic theology. Ezekiel, Deutero-Isaiah and Ezra are later examples of the solitary individuals who pioneered new paths for Israel's religion.

All this means that individuals play an important role in the history of Israelite religion: they represent a distinctive form of Yahweh religion which is not always recognized. In describing developments in the history of Israelite religion, we must always be aware of the interaction between the religious structures indicated on pp. 116ff. and the impulses proceeding from individual figures.

The points of view put forward above are sometimes played off against one another. In the discussion about the role played by Moses in

Israelite religion, Klaus Koch, for example, has talked provocatively about the 'death of the founder of the religion', stressing the historical development of Yahweh religion, which had evolved out of different roots. He held that the historical development of the religion as such had the character of revelation. F. Baumgärtel has energetically opposed this view: the faith of the Old Testament, with its stress on the personal claim on men, was, he believed, inconceivable without the personal revelation made to Moses. Proper scholarly research will not give primacy to either point of view in examining the history of Israelite religion.

The main periods in the history of Israelite religion

The development of Israelite religion was stamped by two epoch-making events, the beginning and the end of Israel as a nation. Through the formation of the nation Israel first became a people; as Israel's tribes grew up, conflicts with their enemies led to a consciousness that they themselves belonged closely together under the guardianship of Yahweh. And the building of a political unity under David completed this national consciousness, with which Yahweh was inseparably bound up.

The roots of Israel's religion can be brought to light more or less clearly by the process of historical reconstruction. This reveals a multiplicity of contradictory religious structures, out of which the Yahweh religion of the later people of Israel was to emerge. At all events, one cannot yet talk here about the real religion of Israel, since Israel did not yet exist as a people. Only a very few Old Testament passages can perhaps be interpreted as the authentic expression of a faith in Yahweh which had not yet taken root in the sphere of a developing or already developed consciousness of Israel as a unified people; we might think of the Song of Miriam in Ex. 15.21, for example, or the battle-cry of the Amalekites in Ex. 17.16. The stories about the earliest period which have been handed down in the Old Testament show the impress of Israel's later unity to a very considerable degree.

Accordingly we could speak of a 'pre-history' of Israelite religion (its heterogeneous roots, which must be deduced hypothetically, are: nature, the religion of the fathers, the pre-Israelite Yahweh religion, Canaanite religion, further elements of tribal religions); and we might distinguish between it and the real history of Israel's religion, which emerges with the coming into being of the nation, and thus with the syncretism of the different religious factors.

The *national period* of Israel's religious history is characterized by the fact that Yahweh religion is always related to the people of Israel in its actual, immediate historical conditions. It is therefore a 'state' religion, comparable with the national religions of Israel's neighbours. The individual is bound to Yahweh by a relationship which simultaneously incorporates him in the community, in his people. The salvation of the individual which is expected from Yahweh is inconceivable without the salvation of the whole nation. The benefits of salvation are primarily meant for the community, and are offered in quite tangible terms: material prosperity, happiness and good fortune in the natural and historical spheres of life, a harmonious development in the life of the community, and success in warding off danger which might prove a threat to this harmony. When the prophets specify what is upsetting the orderly structure, and are thereby forced to predict the disaster which is about to burst upon their hearers, the doom again affects the whole nation, even when the guilt is at most to be ascribed to only a certain section of the people. It is true that the first hints that this collective consciousness could be called in question are heard when, now and again, there is talk of a differentiation in the coming disaster: that it will affect the guilty more than others, so that a *portion* of the nation can be given the prospect of survival and a new beginning. Even the prophets themselves, in their unconventional judgment of the situation, signalized the dawn of an individual experience and thought, which bursts asunder the framework of general perceptions and sentiments.

The period when Israel has ceased to be a nation brings decisive changes. For the historian of religion, the most astonishing phenomenon to follow the destruction of Jerusalem and the collapse of Israel as a political power is the vigour with which Yahweh religion continued to exist. It would have seemed much more likely that the Israelites – especially those living in exile – should have taken over foreign religions. Instead, Yahweh religion acquires immense impetus, creates completely new structures of faith, and becomes to a pre-eminent degree the factor that creates a community outside the political sphere. Religious community and political community are thus no longer identical powers; and here indeed is a problem for Israelite faith which has remained unsolved down to the present day; for the relationship between the community of faith and the political community has never been finally determined in terms that are generally binding.

Two new main trends in Yahweh religion mark the post-exilic period: the development of *eschatology* and the sense of the *individual*:

The way in which the term 'eschatology' is applied varies to a confusing degree. Actually the word means 'doctrine of the last things', i.e., what is ultimate, both chronologically and in significance. One can talk about eschatology when what is actually present is understood as being provisional and to be abolished by a reality still to come. We should not therefore term every expectation of the future eschatological. The classical pre-exilic prophets, for example, lived in expectation of some future act on the part of Yahweh; but they do not await any events which in principle go beyond the horizon of present experience. Their expectation of the future cannot therefore be called eschatological.

The prophet Deutero-Isaiah (Isa. 40-55) takes up the message of the classical prophets, but from a different point of view; guilt is expiated, transgressions against Yahweh's order have been avenged – and indeed doubly so. Consequently an era of salvation can now dawn once more. The qualities of salvation in Deutero-Isaiah considerably exceed anything that was familiar to the Israelites as the 'normal' experience of salvation. True, the usual ideas, familiar from the cult, are taken over, but they are elaborated in a new way (cf. p. 89 above). The salvation proclaimed has the features of paradise: the exiled Israelites, together with Yahweh, are to return to Jerusalem in a triumphal procession, there to enter on a life never before conceivable.

The events following the exile did not fulfil these hopes. There was a movement towards return among the exiles, but it was probably relatively modest. There was certainly no trace of the new quality of life and salvation that had been predicted. None the less, the eschatological expectations remained in existence; the prophecy of Deutero-Isaiah found successors. Finally hopes of this kind were given an important place in apocalyptic; here eschatology is linked with cosmological speculations, with reflections about the law, and so forth (cf. pp. 137ff.).

The emergence of the individual seems to be part of a deliberate programme in Ezekiel. He denies energetically that the people as a whole has a single destiny. Everyone is responsible for himself before Yahweh; his fate depends solely on his behaviour; collective behaviour and collective destiny are put aside as mental categories belonging to the past. In order to belong to Yahweh, ethnic membership of the people of Israel is not enough. What counts is an obedient decision to obey Yahweh's commandments. Thus within Israel itself a dividing line is drawn between those who belong to Yahweh and those who are far from him. Yahweh's will (and his commandments) effects the distinction. Consequently the different expressions of Yahweh's will familiar from the past are gathered together and systematically arranged; out of a multiplicity of commandments comes the law. It is significant that the concept of the *tōrāh*, which originally related to the individual priestly precept from Yahweh as it concerned a particular case (p. 77), now begins to mean this timeless, comprehensive system of a divine expression of will. God reveals himself and rules in the gift of his law (though here different stresses were no doubt possible – more weight could be laid either on the cultic or on the ethical side of the law); to serve Yahweh means to remember and obey this law. The law is therefore no longer self-evident, the undisputed order of nature and people within which pre-exilic Israel had moved.

The evaluation of the different eras varies. We have already mentioned the predilection of modern German scholarship for the prehistory of Israelite religion (pp. 104f.); scholars believed that here the specifically Israelite character could be grasped in its purest form (of course, leaving the Canaanite roots on one side). Here latent aspects of romanticism no doubt play their part; the beginnings are regarded as the unadulterated primal expression of faith in Yahweh (this was already Wellhausen's view, cf. pp. 11f.). The value to be ascribed to the post-exilic period is discussed with particular vigour. Is the concentration on the law and on apocalyptic and eschatological schemes a perverted petrification of Israelite religion, with all its earlier vitality? Wellhausen's views at least continue to exert a strong influence down to the present day. On the other hand, it has been stressed that apocalyptic in particular opens up a new and comprehensive range of theological language, which embraces the world as a whole.

The ambiguity of the religious development of Israel and early Christianity

The tensions which accompanied the progress of the history of Israelite religion have already been mentioned. There were always different tendencies running parallel to one another and these were often mutually exclusive. The sharpest conflicts developed at the very point where individual figures expressed faith in Yahweh with a particular personal stamp. The individual prophets generally stood in opposition to officially organized religion; in one case (Jer. 26.20ff.) we even know of the murder of a prophet (though we otherwise know nothing about him).

The tensions in Israelite religion even affected themes which seem to the reader of the Old Testament to be the unmistakable characteristics of the Old Testament faith, e.g. the exclusiveness of Yahweh worship. For according to information deriving from different periods and spheres, it seems to have been usual in some quarters to worship a female deity as well. That this was quite reconcilable with Yahweh faith is shown by documents from Elephantine, a fifth-century Jewish military colony on an island in the Nile near Asswan. Here there was a temple dedicated to Yahweh in which not only Yahweh himself was worshipped but his wife and a third god as well. We must not push this aside too hastily as a heathen perversion of the true religion of Yahweh; the names of the goddess are derived from the Canaanite home of the Jewish soldiers who were settled there. Apparently a tendency was established which also existed in Israel itself, but was repressed there. The Old Testament contains only one section of the whole breadth of Israel's religion. Everything which was too repugnant has been excluded, or appears as idolatry – as apostasy towards Yahweh.

The wide range of Israelite religion was without doubt narrowed down in the developments which followed the exile. The process whereby particular writings were admitted into the canon is a

clear sign of this. Admittedly, the process of selection and concentration led to no completely unambiguous result. Thus apocalyptic theology, for example, is clearly represented in the Old
Testament canon (above all with Daniel, Isa. 24-27, and other
additions in the prophetic books, though only sparsely). The greater
part of apocalyptic literature has not been accepted as canonical.
Orthodox Judaism concentrates its theological endeavours primarily
on the law and its interpretation, not on cosmological schemes,
though the expectation of the future plays a notable part even in
rabbinic orthodoxy. At all events, Israelite religion at the time of
Jesus – i.e. before the formation of the canon was complete – is
still full of different possible modes of faith. Seen from the perspective of the history of religion, early Christianity can at first be
understood quite well in the framework of Judaism. Jesus appears
as the founder of a splinter group, just as there had been other
groups with their teachers; according to everything that we can
deduce from the New Testament, he was not thinking of forming
a 'new religion' or a 'church'. He ministered and taught entirely
in the light of the faith of the Old Testament, to a great extent
picking up the impulses of prophecy and wisdom, though centring
his message in a unique way on his own person. Christianity thus
appears as *one* possible organic continuation of the Old Testament
development. Other varieties stand beside it, for example the
rabbinic Judaism which led on to orthodoxy.

What is very striking is that the multiplicity and variety of
tension which is characteristic of Israel's religion continues to exist
in Christianity. The events to which the New Testament bears
witness are at first caught up into the different and partly contradictory forms of Israelite religion; categories which were non-
Israelite in origin were added later.

2. *Fields of Experience in the Religion of Yahweh*

In our own century, the tasks for a theology of the Old Testament
have been formulated in very different ways. The following trends can
be observed.

(*a*) Old Testament theology is the equivalent of the history of

Israelite religion. This view had great weight at the beginning of the century and has constantly found supporters ever since.

(*b*) In the multiplicity of historical developments in the Old Testament, the theology of the Old Testament seeks the fundamental ideas which continued to endure in the New Testament and which are ultimately constitutive for today's faith also. The historic witnesses of Old Testament religion are therefore viewed as variations and crystallizations of these basic ideas, which are described systematically (i.e. not in their historical development). Admittedly, the basic ideas which are then claimed seem very pale and abstract. L. Köhler, for example, writes: 'That God is the sovereign Lord is the single and fundamental precept of Old Testament theology' (*Theologie des Alten Testaments*, p. 12). G. Fohrer supplements this: 'The lordship of God and community between God and man' (*Theologische Grundstrukturen des AT*, 1972, p. 98). According to this view, it is the development (and perhaps also the distortion) of this fundamental idea that is to be seen in the history of the Old Testament.

(*c*) Old Testament theology waives all claim to construct a 'centre', a basic idea of the Old Testament. In close co-operation with the history of Israel's religion, it works out the different forms of Old Testament belief in Yahweh. Here, therefore, the theme is the actual variety of the historical developments of Yahweh religion and not a hypothetical basic idea of it. The ordering of the material, and its simultaneous evaluation, starts from a particular premise: that the history of Old Testament faith finds its legitimate continuation in the New Testament's faith in Christ, and is therefore also relevant for Christian faith today. To this extent Old Testament theology is different from the history of Israelite religion, which adopts a less rigid standpoint in its approach and must therefore arrive at more reserved judgments (although of course it cannot get along without them). In what follows we shall indicate some of the essential fields of experience in the faith of the Old Testament – that is to say, we shall be dealing with elements of Old Testament theology. On the relationship between the faiths of Old and New Testaments cf. pp. 143ff. below.

Israel's primary experiences with Yahweh

It is significant that the best known genre from the period in which Israel grew into a national unity and learnt to know Yahweh as her guardian deity and guide is the saga. In all the various kinds of

saga (patriarchal sagas, tribal sagas, etc.) Yahweh plays a central
role (it is only very seldom that the subject is a purely human event,
without Yahweh's participation: Judg. 8.4-21 is an example). Generally, therefore, the sagas are given a 'Yahwistic colouring', they
are theologized; the statements, that is to say, are directed towards
the mutual interaction of Yahweh's behaviour and the behaviour of
the people who have to do with him. Though the sagas originally
touched only on smaller groups (clan, tribe, etc.), they apparently
took on significance for the whole of Israel quite early – e.g. through
the inclusion of the different patriarchs in a single genealogical
pattern.

As we saw on pp. 49ff., the sagas tell of events which give their
stamp to the present and which lead their hearers into particular
attitudes towards spheres of present-day life. As a genre, however,
the saga is not bound to particular institutions, such as the cult.
At a very early period (from the settlement onwards) it already seems
to have been a popular instrument, known all over Israel, for passing
on the constitutive historical experiences with Yahweh.

In later times (to some extent also in connection with the collecting of the sagas and giving them a fixed written form), the ancient
sagas went through a process of theological editing, through the
medium of an accepted theological terminology. This can be shown
particularly clearly, for example, through an investigation of the
transmission history of the sagas contained in the book of Judges.
The formation of the sagas has therefore led to a deliberately
pointed theological interpretation and writing of history, though
this no longer seems to have been 'popular' in the sense that the
individual sagas were 'popular' in the early stage of their transmission. Here we find indications of the opinions of theological
'schools' – perhaps those belonging to particular prophetic or Deuteronomistic trends.

At all events, the idea is preserved throughout that Yahweh
determines the present by his activity in the past. In the patriarchal
and tribal sagas (which originally went back to particular clans and
groups, but were then transferred to the whole of Israel), the
evolution of the Israelite national consciousness finds expression.
And just as Yahweh generally plays a central role in the sagas,

so Israel cannot think of itself as a nation without Yahweh. The fact that Yahweh, and Yahweh alone, is Israel's God, and that Israel is Yahweh's people, is here related and anchored in the hearer's consciousness through definite events which determine the present. This basic theme can be illustrated in concrete terms in various directions; God's acts of judgment towards mankind (Gen. 11.1-9), his protective guidance of the patriarchs (Gen. 12.10-20), his revelation at a particular place and the cult that springs from it (Gen. 28.10-22), his help in time of war through the medium of the first of the kings (I Sam. 11.1-11, 15) – all these are variations on the theme.

The fact that the telling of these sagas in Israel had a quite essential function for faith distinguishes Israel fundamentally from the religions of its neighbours, according to all that we know of them. Their cultic genres (and myth in particular) are the medium *par excellence* through which God is presented verbally.

The law established by Yahweh

Even if one adopts a critical attitude towards the theory of the cultic setting of the apodictic commandments in the framework of an ancient Israelite amphictyony, it is none the less clear that the religion of Yahweh was linked at a very early period with particular demands for modes of behaviour which were of unqualified validity. We must remember here that even in the time before the worship of Yahweh, Israelite groups were familiar with sentences of the 'Thou shalt not ...' type (cf. p. 75). The relationship to Yahweh soon also found expression in sentences of this kind – sentences which enunciate the fundamental norms which make human life possible. In the Decalogue, the norms which affect the relationship to Yahweh and those which regulate the common life of man with man are linked together.

The date of the Decalogue is much disputed. In its present form, with its articles of unequal length (even if we ignore the later explanatory expansions), some positive and some negative, it seems to show signs of being a secondary composition; what we have here is not in fact an original, unified block of commandments which belong together. Still, we already have in Hos. 4.2, a list of trans-

gressions very similar to that in the Decalogue. Admittedly at this
particular point only transgressions in the sphere of man's common
life are mentioned, although Hosea's message is coloured through
and through by the first commandment, and the second commandment also plays an essential role for him. On the whole, it is
clear that in Hosea the fundamental norms to be observed in
behaviour to God and within human society form an indistinguish-
able totality.

The absolute age of the first and second commandments cannot
be determined with certainty. In the pre-exilic period at least the
prohibition of the worship of other gods is not to be misunderstood
as being a theoretical demand for monotheism. The existence of
other gods is assumed everywhere; but for Israel the only one who
can count is Yahweh. This corresponds to the experience expressed
in the sagas; it is only through the acts of Yahweh that Israel can
understand itself as a people. Thus the first commandment con-
forms to Israel's constitutive experience with Yahweh; the date
when the corresponding apodictic formulation was arrived at can
be established less precisely.

The second commandment presents greater difficulty. Apparently the
short original form of the commandment demanded a general renun-
ciation of images in the cult of Yahweh, which was by no means a
matter of course in the early period (cf. the unabashed description in
Judg. 8.24-27a, where the making of an image is described: 27b is the
reaction of a later period which knew the second commandment; see
further Judg. 17f.). It is hard to escape the impression that the second
commandment only grew up in the course of time. What is the function
of a divine image? It is an actualization of God's presence, a medium of
the holy. Association with the image of a god allows participation in that
god's power: the misunderstanding that God and the image were identical undoubtedly arose here and there. It is quite conceivable that it was
only in the course of time that the religion of Yahweh arrived at the
insight that Yahweh was irreconcilable with images of the divine (and
not only with misunderstood ones). The accessibility of the god in the
image contradicted Israel's fundamental experiences with Yahweh, who
remained Israel's Lord even when he was the being who was far from
her: for example, in his refusal of aid. For the attribution of the commandments to Moses, cf. p. 121.

In the course of Israel's history, more and more weight was laid on the expression of Yahweh's will in commandments. From the time of Deuteronomy onwards, the commandments were brought into systematic correlation with the theme of Yahweh's guidance in history, cf. pp. 136ff.

The cult of Yahweh

Like the cults of Israel's neighbours, the cult of Yahweh first takes its bearing from nature in the period of the monarchy. The great feasts – the feast of unleavened bread, the feast of weeks, the autumn festival – mark especially important parts of the farmer's year (the cutting of the first barley and the enjoyment of the unleavened bread made from it; the end of the corn harvest, with the presentation of the 'firstfruits', the feast of ingathering, particularly the harvest of grapes and olives). These were pilgrimage festivals: the farmers had to visit the sanctuary (cf. what are presumably the oldest brief instructions for these feasts, Ex. 23.14ff.). Here in the cult Israel experienced Yahweh as the Lord of fertility, who looked after the order of nature, with its annual cycle.

Whereas the roots of the cult in the cyclical progress of nature are clearly evident in the legal texts, not much of this is to be traced in Israel's cultic literature. Here it becomes obvious that the order of salvation manifested in the cult reaches far beyond nature. God's creation certainly affects nature and its fertility as well (see for example Ps. 65.9ff.), but beyond that it touches the whole realm of Israel's social and political existence. (Incidentally, creation appears in very different aspects, in the struggle with chaos as well as in sovereign and indisputed decree; cf. for example Ps. 89.9ff., compared with Ps. 19.1-6.) The intercessions for the king, such as Pss. 72; 20; 21, show how much in pre-exilic times the securing of natural fertility, the establishment of peace abroad (or, it might be, a victorious defensive war) and the preservation of a just social life with fair shares for all were elements of a comprehensive order which had its origin in the cult and had to be put into practice by the king. Nature and history are different aspects of the *one* order, which is experienced in concentrated form in the cult and which finds concrete expression in the most varied spheres of life. The fundamental rhythm of this cult is the annual repetition, the yearly renewal of the archetypal order; in the cult, life is called back to its origins; it appears anew as Yahweh's creation. That is why the psalms talk about the 'eternal life' and the 'eternal rule' of the king, who is even termed 'god' (cf. Ps. 21.4, 6; 45.6); the king's function is everlasting in so far as it represents and realizes in Israel Yahweh's most essentially characteristic actions, which are visible in the cult. On the other hand, it is often stressed that there is a fundamental distinction between king and God; but the 'divinity' of the king will have been judged differently at different times in the pre-exilic period. Sooner or later the specific events which were constitutive of Israel's historical existence (the exodus, the settlement in the promised land, etc.) became complexes of cultic tradition. The great feasts are given a historical justification. In this way Israel actualized in yearly repetition Yahweh's fundamental past acts of salvation.

Attention should be drawn to some special features which emerge from a comparison between the cult of Yahweh and the cults of Israel's neighbours. First of all, it is noticeable that the Old Testament texts term Yahweh the sole God, with whom alone the people have to do in cultic ceremonies. Even where ideas of a pantheon can still be detected, this pantheon has no significance of its own beside Yahweh. In particular, the texts do not mention any goddess. This is probably one reason why sexual practices play no part in the cult; no *hieros gamos* (sacred marriage) is mentioned in the texts. Yahweh provides for fertility, but he is not himself part of the power of fertility, nor is he its embodiment. The distance between Creator and creation is felt more strongly here than elsewhere. The realm of death is completely excluded from the cult. Yahweh has nothing to do with death, and the dead have nothing to do with Yahweh. Perhaps the themes of 'living and dying' were so bound up with the notion of the living and dying of the god that Israel – which was quite incapable of thinking of Yahweh as the dying God, stripped of all his power – kept Yahweh and the realm of the dead strictly apart.

We must once again point out that the genre of myth is absent from the Old Testament. In a reflection of man's astonishment and gratitude, the hymn tells of Yahweh's acts and his manifold decrees. This points to the fact that in Israel the function of the cult is much less that of creating reality than is the case elsewhere. For Israel, the way was pointed towards an experience of Yahweh outside the cult – experience which the cult presented in concentrated form and committed to language. This is one reason why Ps. 132, for example, preserves the remembrance of the historical circumstances which led to the founding of the cult of Yahweh in Jerusalem. A historical event and not a divine drama stands at the beginning.

It is hardly conceivable that all these particular features of Israel's cult existed in this form from the beginning of the period of the monarchy. It is historically far more probable that they evolved slowly in the course of Israel's development. The Old Testament texts have most probably been 'cleansed' of ideas which were different in kind (cf. pp. 126f.).

Yahweh and wisdom

We have already discussed the concerns of wisdom in the course of our study of genres. Wisdom seeks to grasp in words the structure inherent in the world, with all its diversity and even its contradictions, and both to express it and control it; the aim is then to initiate man into this order, so that he is upheld and invigorated by it. Here the concentration on the world of men is typical of Israel. The fitting of the human order into a cosmos which also embraces nature has almost disappeared from the texts which have come down to us, though we must assume that attempts of this kind were made in the early period of Israelite wisdom (cf. pp. 182f.).

There is still the question of the relationship between wisdom and history, and especially between Israelite wisdom and the history which Yahweh brought about on Israel's behalf. First of all we must stress once more that the order which emerges in wisdom is not a closed structure, a rigid system (at least in its original intention; of course it happens again and again – and particularly in Israel! – that for example the connection between action and consequence turns into a dogma which does not require verification but takes precedence over experience, thus leading to a mode of existence remote from reality). In its original strivings, wisdom is open to every new experience; a saying which ceases to be confirmed by experience is forgotten. In this way wisdom can adapt itself to new historical situations. But it always consists of typical constellations which recur continually. What is missing is observation of the unique, irreplaceable historical event. And this means that the distinction between present and past is missing too.

Now it is highly significant in Israel's development that the traditional sagas were accepted into wisdom. The most characteristic example is the Court History of David (II Sam. 9-20; I Kings 1-2; it probably already begins in II Sam. 6.20ff., where it is linked with the story of the ark). At first sight the narrative appears to be an extensive family chronicle. It begins with the childlessness of Michal, David's wife, who, as a daughter of Israel's first king, Saul, would have been best fitted to bear the heir to the throne. Various episodes follow, affecting the relationship between David and his children, until finally – after a multiplicity of complications, intrigues, conflicts and violence – Solomon ascends the throne and eliminates his rivals. This family chronicle of course describes events which were of considerable political relevance for the time, and the historical circumstances, as well as the sequence, of David's family history are carefully preserved.

It is noticeable that in the description of the characters involved, positive or negative characteristics of wisdom come into play again and again; the details of the events reported should probably also be viewed as embodying the themes of wisdom thinking rather than historical happenings. In this way the family chronicle has become stylized into a model of a sequence of events interpreted in the light of wisdom.

God is seldom mentioned – but when he is mentioned at all it is at decisive points. He does not intervene directly in events, but his providence and ordering powers form the background against which the human events are acted out: David's murder of one of his servants, carried out to cover up his adulterous relations with the man's wife, displeases Yahweh – the consequence is disaster for David: the child who is born to him dies (II Sam. 11.27). About Solomon, the woman's second child, we are told simply, 'Yahweh

loved him' (II Sam. 12.24). With this, the key is already set for
further events. And finally Yahweh sees to it that a wise piece of
advice given to David's stupidly arrogant son, who has rebelled
against his father, is not followed (II Sam. 17.14), with corresponding results.

In ways like these, the saga, when adopted into the realm of
wisdom thinking, has turned into real historiography. The point
of departure for the account is still the family; but the acute observation of the processes involved and the interpretation of events are
due to the way wisdom looks at things. In this way, the eye for
what is historically unique has become keener. Yahweh appears
as the one who shapes unique historical processes from behind the
scenes.

*The mutual interpenetration of different fields of experience of
Yahweh*

We have already mentioned several times that in the evolution of
the religion of Yahweh different spheres of experience and thinking
are moulded together in a coherent whole. Particular experiences
of God and the world are in this way extended and strive towards
a totality: the *whole* of reality is to be confronted with the *one*
Yahweh. We shall now look at the way in which this tendency
manifests itself in three forms of Old Testament faith.

(a) Classical prophecy. For the prophets, Yahweh's expression
of his will is of prime importance. But the spheres of his demands
presented by the prophets are quite different. Hosea is primarily
concerned with the sole and proper worship of Yahweh; Isaiah
scourges the perversion of the urban social order, which does not
allow everyone his proper place, but is misused by the strong for
the suppression and exploitation of the helpless. The characteristics
of Yahweh known from the cult are taken up by the prophets;
Hosea describes Yahweh as the God of fertility (e.g. 2.12ff.), and in
a similar way Isaiah picks up the Jerusalem cultic tradition in a
positive sense. But at the same time both prophets – each in his
own way – indicated the point at which the cult becomes empty,
a senseless farce; and this point is reached when Yahweh's funda-

mental demands are ignored. Finally, for both prophets it is a matter of course that the guilt which they have laid bare will come to fruition in the political and historical sphere.

Two things emerge from the prophets: on the one hand there is a clarification of the spheres in which Israel came to experience Yahweh and they are thought of as a single whole; on the other hand, the significance of the different experiences of Yahweh is brought to expression with a ruthlessness to which the prophets' contemporaries were unused. This explains the isolation of these prophets. The individual elements of their message are not new – they are ideas which were current in the Israelite religion of that time. What is new is the fusing together of these elements into an unprecedented totality. The God of the prophets is thus marked, not by particular characteristics unknown to Israel, but by the unqualified nature and universality of his claim, which calls in question the whole relationship to Israel up to that point.

It is in the light of all this that the prediction of disaster made by these prophets is to be understood. Israel cannot satisfy Yahweh's claim as the prophets experience it. As a consequence of this insight, the dark perspective of the future emerges. Of course, this very expectation of an act of Yahweh's, still to come in its totality, opens up a new sphere for Israel's faith: the future hope. In Hosea and Isaiah it is clear from time to time that in the process of judgment Yahweh will simultaneously proceed to establish his will for salvation in its entirety.

(b) Deuteronomy and the Deuteronomistic movement. We also find this comprehensive view of the different realms of experience which are relevant for the religion of Yahweh in Deuteronomy, and in the associated theological movement which finds expression in many of the Old Testament books (cf. pp. 20f.). Here the prophetic proclamation is taken further in a particular way. Yahweh's guidance in history and, correspondingly, Israel's destiny are closely linked with the order of life established by Yahweh and marked out by the commandments. Israel's attitude towards the commandments has a direct effect on the life of the nation – as a blessing or a curse: turning away from Yahweh (the first commandment stands in the

centre; the others almost seem like a mere exposition of this main commandment) brings about disaster in all sectors of life – in the natural, social and political dimensions of Israel's existence. The glance back at Israel's history is used to light up the decision with which the Israel of the present sees itself faced: the decision for Yahweh or against him. Since time immemorial, his guidance has opened up for Israel the possibility of life as blessing. Israel has always had the chance to choose life or, in disobedience, to go on to destruction – and often enough it chose the latter possibility. In this comprehensive theological outline the cult, too, has its important function; for in the cult the unity and purity of the worship of Yahweh comes most clearly to expression (correspondingly, apostasy from Yahweh is also seen in its crassest form in the cult of strange gods). The most widely varying forms of speech and thought have been placed at the service of this theological conception: saga, homily, the reflections of wisdom and cultic poetry.

Deuteronomic and Deuteronomistic theology ultimately confront Israel with an alternative: to be a people with Yahweh, or without Yahweh to abandon its existence. This theological approach is inconceivable without the prophetic proclamation which preceded it. Its setting is the moment when Israel's national existence was most endangered – perhaps shortly before the exile, and at all events during the exilic period.

(c) Apocalyptic. A further comprehensive attempt to integrate the different fields of experience of Yahweh in a single unity can be found in apocalyptic.

In the context of the late Old Testament, Jewish and early Christian periods, apocalyptic means both a particular theological movement and its specific literary expression. The apocalyptist expresses himself in the literary form of revelation, the content of which is frequently the description of a vision. Interpretation of the vision and its revelation – more or less clearly indicated in the vision itself – allows the apocalyptist's proclamation to be introduced.

The apocalyptist is silent about his own name and about his historical setting. He hides behind the authority of well-known sages who lived in bygone times: Daniel, Enoch, etc. This is in itself indicative of the fact that the apocalyptist sees his situation in a broad historical context.

The fundamental experience of apocalyptic is that of the hidden nature of God. God's people, Israel, has not been restored to existence since the exile; Yahweh's guiding hand in history is not visible from historical events. Israel is the plaything of the empires of the Ancient East. Yahweh's law is not generally observed, and the consequence is evident. The forces of disorder, the powers of chaos, at present have the upper hand.

But the apocalyptist is able to see through this situation. He realizes that the lordship of Yahweh has not been abolished, but is about to be established finally in the near future. Here the hope of eschatological prophecy is carried through to the end (cf. pp. 124f.). This belief finds its expression in the 'revelations' already mentioned. Widely though the ideas vary, sometimes contradicting one another, they none the less display a number of constant basic features.

The first characteristic feature of the apocalyptic schemes is that even the apparent disorder of the present is part of a hidden order – an order which finds a fixed, chronological development. The dominance of the forces of chaos develops in world history according to plan (it is usual to talk of apocalyptic determinism here); the wise man is capable of judging the stage that the development has reached from the knowledge revealed to him. Here, therefore, wisdom no longer has anything to do with a universal order which is obvious and understandable to all; the knowledge that is now necessary is the product of supernatural inspiration. World history moves in the direction of a complete revolution when Yahweh will establish his power and will destroy the forces of chaos; and then his newly created order will be visible to all. It is natural that the ancient images about the struggle with chaos should take on new actuality here. God's victory over his enemies has almost the same meaning for the apocalyptist as for the participator in the cultic ritual of the struggle with chaos; only the apocalyptist does not live in the cyclical experience of this saving event – he expects it as a unique happening in the future (cf. pp. 40f., 54f., 98). A distinction is often made between 'national' and 'cosmic' eschatology, which are said to be found in different apocalyptic trends, but this is purely relative; the single order which the apocalyptist expects (and which had earlier been experienced as a reality in the cult) embraces both nature and political reality. Stress on the different aspects can, however, shift. In the light of all this the dualism of apocalyptic is also understandable. The present time, dominated by the rule of chaos, is contrasted with the coming time, which will see the lordship of God. There is an irresolvable contradiction here: in the present *only* the lordship of evil is at work (albeit within the limits of the development determined by God), and God's sovereignty will openly exert its power *only* in the coming time of salvation. Accordingly the devout man suffers in the present; he clings to the law in the hope of a coming revolution.

The apocalyptic schemes witness to a theology which had lost sight of the visible proofs of divine activity. In spite of that, it clings to the certainty that God is responsible for every sphere of life, and especially for the course of history. In this way themes handled by prophecy and by Deuteronomic and Deuteronomistic theology are picked up once more and freshly assimilated in a new and difficult age.

3. The Relationship between the Testaments as a Problem in Systematic Theology

The complementary relationship between Old and New Testaments

At certain points in the New Testament we already find reflections about the relationship between the events of the Old Testament and the Christ event. Two main ways of finding a relationship between the two testaments are possible: the idea of the fulfilment of prophecy, and typology.

The first of these two ideas proceeds from the premise that the Old Testament contains a series of passages which point towards an event in a future beyond the Old Testament itself. Jesus appears as the saviour of Israel and the world whose coming is already announced in the Old Testament. According to this view, some parts of the Old Testament cannot be understood by themselves, because the prophecies are only fulfilled in the Christ event. Yet the New Testament application of Old Testament passages does not do justice to their original meaning (for example, in the case of the Messianic promises, which originally referred to a kingly office in the political sense). The viewpoint of the New Testament writers is stamped by their present experience of Christ, which also explains the freedom with which Old Testament texts are handled. The Old Testament context plays no role. Sometimes different quotations are combined or altered. The only essential is that some feature of the Christ event can be understood as being the consummation of an Old Testament promise.

Typology established that an Old Testament event can be repeated and heightened in the New. Thus Paul, for example, compares Israel's situation in the wilderness with the position of Christians (I Cor. 10.1-13), using it to describe the situation between temptation and the turning to Christ.

In a great many passages we find neither a real relationship between prophecy and fulfilment, nor a typological one. Instead of that the New Testament events are simply framed in images, thought-categories and language drawn from the Old Testament. This does nothing to explain the connection between Old Testament and New Testament events, but it preserves the solidarity between the two: the New Testament writer experiences a unity between the Christ event and God's acts in the Old Testament which is a matter of course for him and needs no preliminary explanation.

The intention behind these modes of interpretation is theologically relevant, even though an investigation of the texts by the methods of historical criticism cannot ratify their New Testament application in detail. They take their proper place when the irrelinquishable connection between the happenings of Old and New Testaments is given theological expression.

G. von Rad makes an important contribution to this problem in his *Old Testament Theology*. He determines the relationship between the Old and New Testaments as being one of *transmission history*. Transmission history already plays a prominent part in his account of the nature of Old Testament faith. Von Rad describes how, in the Old Testament, faith again and again learns to know Yahweh's acts anew, adapts to changed situations, and thus always thrusts forward to a new verbal grasp of the relationship to Yahweh. Prophecy has a special function in this development. It achieves the insight that Yahweh's actions as they affect his main concern are still in the future. In this way the horizon of expectation in Yahweh religion enters particularly clearly into the consciousness of Israel's faith.

The New Testament lives from the consciousness that these expectations have come to fulfilment in Christ. The Christ event is on the one hand experienced as something completely new, different from everything known hitherto; yet it is only conceivable at all in the framework of the Old Testament expectation. 'Israel's history with God thrusts forward violently into the future, and in the New Testament this phenomenon of ever more powerfully concentrated expectation appears in a new light; for there, following upon the numerous earlier new saving beginnings, it reaches its last hermeneutical modification and its full and final interpretation' (*Old Testament Theology II*, p. 332).

In this sense the New Testament can be understood as a new interpretation of the history of Old Testament faith with ultimate validity; where the Old Testament can tell of many different happenings in which Yahweh proved himself as God to his people, the New Testament tells of *one* final happening, which sets all previous events in their proper light: the ministry, death and resurrection of Jesus. The vast breadth of Yahweh religion, with all its tensions, is given its goal in the Christ event.

Consequently, in any interpretation of biblical events, two perspectives must always be parallel and in correlation: on the one hand an enquiry into the development of Israel's faith from its beginnings down to the faith of the New Testament (for the meaning of Jesus can only be understood in the sphere of understanding opened up by the developments in the Old Testament); on the other hand, an illumination of the multiplicity of Israel's modes of belief in the light of the New Testament (for in this context they are given a certain direction and clarity). In this way Old and New Testament happenings appear as *one* indissoluble coherent structure in which the Christ event represents the final happening in the divine history.

Now of course it must be remembered that the New Testament makes use of the Old Testament in different ways, and that there are different types of interpretation of the Christ event. But varied though New Testament theology is, the common ground is none the less clear enough: the premise that God's final activity is bound up with Jesus. New theological outlines must therefore consider the message and fate of Jesus and test themselves against them.

Post-biblical theology has always had to come to terms with constantly new historical situations and intellectual movements, which pose the task of transposing and reinterpreting biblical theology to meet the needs of the altered situation. Both the history of the church and the history of theology can be understood as expressions of this attempt; these are therefore a witness to the continuing process of transmission. But the task of finding the normative centre of this complex of understanding remains unaltered.

The antithetical relationship between Old and New Testament events

The New Testament consistently adheres to the qualitative difference between the manifold saving acts in the Old Testament and the one saving event of the New (thus according to Matt. 21.33ff., for example, Jesus does not simply stand on the same level with the prophets, who are the bearers of revelation in the Old Testament). This difference often plays an important role, too, in the pattern of promise and fulfilment as well as in the typological interpretation of Old Testament passages: all conceivable promises are fulfilled and surpassed in Christ (cf. for example II Cor. 1.21; Matt. 13.17). Moreover, in typological repetitions of Old Testament occurrences, it is often plain that salvation is just what the Old Testament events cannot achieve (e.g. John 6.48ff.); in the Old Testament, accordingly, we find an anti-type of the New Testament event of salvation. The critical comparison of the Old Testament and the New has always played an important role in the church; in extreme cases this has even led to the Old Testament being called in question as Holy Scripture (Marcion rejected it in the second century and his position has constantly found adherents since).

In recent times the contrast between the Old and the New Testament has been stressed with great energy by *Rudolf Bultmann*. He enquires whether the Old Testament as a whole had the character of promise, pointing towards the New Testament, and crystallizes the question in terms which are of essential importance for both Old and New Testaments, and which accordingly are particularly significant for determining the continuity or discontinuity between the events of the two. The themes in question are: covenant, the sovereignty of God and the people of God.

Bultmann establishes that there is an analogous tendency in the way in which the Old Testament develops these three concepts. The 'covenant' applies first of all to the chosen people, Israel; for popular feeling it is a self-evident feature of everyday cultic life. But in prophecy this idea of the covenant reaches a crisis: the prophets lay down conditions for the covenant which in their very nature are incapable of fulfilment by any nation as a whole. Consequently, in prophetic eyes, the covenant loses its validity for contemporary life; it becomes the subject of eschatological expectation – but again as a covenant with the people of Israel as a historic-historical power. Corresponding developments apply to the other two concepts as well.

In this eschatologization Bultmann sees a permanent and inescapable contradiction: the Old Testament development constantly thrusts forward beyond the sphere of this world's experience; the future nature of the benefits of salvation is a sign of this. None the less the categories of thought belonging to the present world are not abandoned; the expected covenant, after all, stands fundamentally on the same basis as the covenant which prophecy has recognized to be ineffective in the present.

Israel comes to grief over the indissoluble nature of this contradiction, and its failure is *the* characteristic mark of its religious development. The contradiction is overcome by the Christ event, which comes to expression in the New Testament: the sphere of the covenant loses its limitations and embraces the whole of mankind; the lordship of Christ loses its worldly connotations, and cannot be depicted in the categories of the earthly exercise of power; the people of God who belong to the new covenant do not represent an empirical historical power, but anyone who is called out of the world through the claim of the gospel and who belongs to the body of Christ is a member of the *ekklesia*.

The Old Testament manifests the failure of human existence. This existence really takes its bearings from God but seeks realization through an independent shaping of secular history. Faith is able to recognize the failure; for faith, the Old Testament strivings towards salvation and the New Testament saving event seem correlated elements which yet stand in inescapable contradiction to one another or, to express it in the categories of Lutheran (and, in germ, even Pauline) theology, they appear as law and gospel. For Bultmann, the Old Testament modes of faith are no more than random examples of human existence under the rule of the law, which stand in what is fundamentally a chance historical relationship to the saving event of the New Testament. The fact that the understanding of this saving event is inescapably dependent on the linguistic sphere of the Old Testament is not taken into consideration by Bultmann.

The stress on the comparison between the saving events of the Old and New Testaments is undoubtedly justified. Through a critical comparison with the Christ event, the provisional nature of the happenings and modes of faith which precede it become evident, as do their limitations. But the same is, of course, true of the New Testament compared with the later tradition: the theological schemes which we meet here are always to be measured critically against their theme, Christ. The ambiguity in the Old Testament message and in the proclamation of the New Testament and the church differ only in so far as the latter, for all its historical relativity, still has as centre a *single* event; whereas the Old Testament, which takes its bearings from different saving events, lacks the single centre and thus remains fundamentally within the framework of its ambiguity. The Christ event cannot be seen in isolation; it is only comprehensible in the setting of the ambiguous revelation of the Old Testament, and it has only been mediated to the present through the transmission of the church; but it forms the central point within the history of faith, standing out in clear relief – the centre which provides the critical yardstick for transmission of that faith.

The comparison of the Christ event and the history of the transmission of the Christian faith has yet another aspect. Christian faith cannot simply interpret itself as stemming from tradition – as being, so to speak, an automatic or chance extension of the transmission of that faith. It knows that it is based on the present call of God, the call of the Christ event in its immediate and present form; and then of course it sees itself set within the sphere of the Christian tradition in its verbal confession of faith and its concrete forms.

Interpreting the biblical texts

In chapters I-III we saw how the different exegetical questions are connected with the trends of thought and theology belonging to the period in which they arose. Every question has its corresponding methodological procedure; that is to say, light is shed on the text in a way which can be identified and traced. In the process of exegesis, therefore, interests and questions which have already taken fixed form are brought to bear on the text, and methodological clarity will guarantee that these questions are consistently carried through and thought out to the end. It would be an error to assume that at any point the text comes to light 'as it really is', in its pure historical past. The interpreter has always long since introduced the questions of his own time into his procedure though perhaps without rendering an account of the fact, because the methodological questions only reflect the interests of a period in a very general and formalized way.

The more varied the methodological aspects through which a scholar approaches a text, the more comprehensively can questions touching today's self-understanding of the world be discussed in dialogue with that text. Methodological narrowness or one-sidedness means that questions which concern the world today are excluded from the viewpoint of the interpretative process.

The theologian's particular dealings with biblical texts are therefore marked first by these methodological aspects, which of course afford perspectives not only on biblical texts but similar on other literary material as well (the form taken by particular approaches is, of course, always influenced by the concern to make the subject-matter accessible to present-day understanding). In theological exegesis, however, there is an additional factor. In the theological exegesis of a biblical text it must be observed that the text and its interpreter are bound together by a coherent structure of language and understanding, which develops in the Old Testament, finds its centre with Jesus, and is then continued in the history of the church; it is this coherent whole which points the way to understanding.

The theologian who is concerned with biblical texts in his church work is as a rule challenged to interpret a text in some specific situation. That is to say, he has to preach; he has to put across a text in teaching young people or adults; in thinking about some ethical problem he sees that he has to go back to a consideration of the biblical texts, etc. That is to say, he is concerned with the quite specific questions and interests of his time and his situation. Moreover, it is a matter of course that these aspects too must be brought into the process of interpretation.

The interpreter must therefore keep a number of different things in mind together: the questions and problems of the particular contemporary situation, which challenges the theologian to come to terms with it; the text in the situation of its own time and in its original intention; the context of the biblical and theological understanding which give text and interpreter their place in the general tradition of Christian theology; finally, a critical comparison with the centre of this complex of understanding which is focussed on Christ. Through the application of different methods of interpretation, a process of thought will be indicated which can generally be followed and which will already span the horizon of our present-day experience of reality. Thus the methods will not prevent the interpreter from drawing the pressing questions of the moment into the process of interpretation; indeed they will help these questions to achieve greater universality and increased persuasiveness. By keeping all these different questions in mind simultaneously, the theologian may expect clarification of the situation which is the starting point of his exegesis; for that situation will now be integrated into a coherent structure of understanding which preserves the intention of biblical theology and is thus open for proclamation and responsible Christian action.

Abbreviations

Bibliographical Note

This book, which was written as a basic textbook for German readers, reflects above all the present state of German Old Testament studies. Further details about particular sections are to be found in the works listed below.

General

H. J. Kraus, *Geschichte der historisch-kritischen Erforschung des Alten Testaments*, ²1969

G. Fohrer, *Introduction to the Old Testament*, SPCK 1970

O. Kaiser, *Einleitung in das Alte Testament*, ²1970

H. Barth – O. H. Steck, *Exegese des Alten Testaments – Leitfaden der Methodik*, ²1971

G. Fohrer et al., *Exegese des Alten Testaments. Einführung in die Methodik*, 1973

K. Koch, *The Growth of the Biblical Tradition*, A. & C. Black 1969

G. Ebeling, 'The Significance of the Critical Historical Method for Church and Theology in Protestantism', in *Word and Faith*, SCM Press 1963, pp. 17-61

G. Sauter, *Vor einem neuen Methodenstreit in der Theologie?*, 1970

For attempts to apply structuralism to Old Testament interpretation see especially W. Richter, *Exegese als Literaturwissenschaft. Entwurf einer alttestamentlichen Literaturtheorie und Methodologie*, 1971; R. Barthes et al., *Analyse structurale et exégèse biblique*, 1971.

There are numerous valuable articles in *Die Religion in Geschichte und Gegenwart*, ³1957ff.

Chapter I

For Wellhausen see also L. Perlitt, *Vatke und Wellhausen*, 1965. Further discussion of Deuteronomy may be found in M. Noth, *Überlieferungs-*

geschichtliche Studien, 1943; G. Seitz, *Redaktionsgeschichtliche Studien zum Deuteronomium*, 1971; of the Elohist in H. W. Wolff, 'Zur Thematik der elohistischen Fragmente im Pentateuch', *EvTh* 29, 1969, pp. 59ff.=*Gesammelte Studien*, ²1973, pp. 402ff.; of the Yahwist in R. Smend, *Die Erzählung des Hexateuch*, 1912; O. Eissfeldt, *Hexateuch-Synopse*, 1922. For the prophets, and particularly Amos, see: J. Wellhausen, *Die kleinen Propheten*, ³1898; H. W. Wolff, *Dodekapropheton* 2, BK XIV, 2, 1969; R. Smend, 'Das Nein des Amos', *EvTh* 23, 1963, pp. 404ff.; S. Amsler, 'Amos, prophète de la onzième heure', *ThZ* 21, 1965, pp. 318ff.; I. Willi-Plein, *Vorformen der Schriftexegese innerhalb des AT*, 1971.

Chapter II

For Gunkel see also W. Klatt, *Hermann Gunkel*, 1969. For form criticism see C. Westermann, 'Arten der Erzählung in der Genesis', in *Forschung am AT*, 1964, pp. 9ff.; id., *Das Loben Gottes in den Psalmen*, ³1963, esp. pp. 48ff.; F. Crüsemann, *Studien zur Formgeschichte von Hymnus und Danklied in Israel*, 1969. For the role of the cultic prophets see F. Stolz, 'Der Streit um die Wirklichkeit in der Sudreichsprophetie des 8. Jahrhunderts', *WuD* 12, 1973, pp. 9ff. For the cult see H.-J. Hermisson, *Sprach und Ritus im altisraelitischen Kult*, 1965; L. Ruppert, 'Psalm 25 und die Grenze kultorientierter Psalmenexegese', *ZAW* 84, 1972, pp. 576ff. Alt's theories are criticized and discussed further in K. Elliger, 'Das Gesetz Leviticus 18', *ZAW* 67, 1955, pp. 1ff=*Kleine Schriften zum AT*, 1966, pp. 232ff.; E. Gerstenberger, *Wesen und Herkunft des apodiktischen Rechtes*, 1965; R. Kilian, 'Apodiktisches und kasuistisches Recht im Lichte ägyptischer Parallelen', *BZ* NF 7, 1963, pp. 185ff.; H. Schulz, *Das Todesrecht im AT*, 1969. See also G. Liedke, *Gestalt und Benennung alttestamentlicher Rechtssätze*, 1971; V. Wagner, *Rechtssätze in gebundener Sprache und Rechtsatzreihen im israelitischen Recht*, 1971. For the priestly Torah see J. Begrich, 'Die priesterliche Tora', *BZAW* 66, 1936, pp. 63ff.=*Gesammelte Studien zum AT*, 1964, pp. 232ff

For wisdom see H. H. Schmid, *Wesen und Geschichte der Weisheit*, 1966; W. Richter, *Recht und Ethos*, 1966; H.-J. Hermisson, *Studien zur israelitischen Spruchweisheit*, 1968; H. W. Wolff, *Amos' geistige Heimat*, 1964; G. von Rad, *Wisdom in Israel*, SCM Press 1972. There are further discussions of prophecy in: C. Westermann, *Basic Forms of Prophetic Speech*, Abingdon Press 1967; G. von Rad, *Old Testament Theology* 2, Oliver and Boyd 1965; W. H. Schmidt, *Zukunftsgewissheit und Gegenwartskritik*, 1973; F. Stolz, 'Aspekte religioser und sozialer Ordnung im alten Israel', *ZEE* 17, 1973, pp. 145ff

Chapter III

Mowinckel's key discussion of the cult is to be found in S. Mowinckel,

Religion und Kultus, 1953; cf. id., *Psalmenstudien* II, 1922. See also
S. G. F. Brandon, 'The Myth and Ritual Position critically considered',
in *Myth, Ritual and Kingship*, ed. S. H. Hooke, OUP 1958, pp. 261ff.;
S. H. Hooke (ed.), *Myth and Ritual*, OUP 1933; *The Labyrinth*, OUP
1935; T. H. Gaster, *Thespis*, New York ²1961; E. Hornung, *Geschichte
als Fest*, 1966; H. H. Schmid, *Gerechtigkeit als Weltordnung*, 1968;
F. Stolz, *Strukturen und Figuren im Kult von Jerusalem*, 1970.

For Noth's theory of the amphictyony see, in addition to the works
mentioned in the text, id., 'Das Amt des "Richters Israels"', *Festschrift
Bertholet*, 1950, pp. 404f.=*Gesammelte Studien* II, 1969, pp. 71ff.; id.,
The History of Israel, A. and C. Black ²1960, pp. 53-138; for criticism,
G. Fohrer, "Amphiktyonie" und "Bund"', *ThLZ* 91, 1966, cols. 801ff.,
893ff. For von Rad's theories see also G. E. Mendenhall, *Law and
Covenant in Israel and the Ancient Near East*, The Biblical Colloquium
1955; H. J. Kraus, *Worship in Israel*, Blackwell 1962; H. Wildberger,
Jahwes Eigentumsvolk, 1960; K. Baltzer, *The Covenant Formulary*,
Fortress Press 1972; W. Beyerlin, *Origins and History of the Oldest
Sinaitic Traditions*, Blackwell 1965; A. Weiser, *Introduction to the
Old Testament*, Darton, Longman and Todd 1961. For criticism see
E. Kutsch, *Verheissung und Gesetz*, 1972; L. Perlitt, *Bundestheologie
im AT*, 1969; L. Rost, 'Das kleine geschichtliche Credo', in *Das kleine
Credo und andere Studien zum AT*, 1965. For the holy war see R.
Smend, *Jahwekrieg und Stämmebund*, ²1966; F. Stolz, *Jahwes und
Israels Kriege*, 1972.

Prophecy and the cult are discussed in G. von Rad, 'Die falschen
Propheten', *ZAW* 51, 1933, pp. 109ff.=*Gesammelte Studien* II, 1973,
pp. 212ff.; E. Würthwein, 'Amos-Studien', *ZAW* 62, 1949/50, pp. 10ff.;
id., 'Der Ursprung der prophetischen Gerichtsrede', *ZThK* 49, 1952, pp.
1ff.; H. Graf Reventlow, *Das Amt des Propheten bei Amos*, 1962 (and
other studies).

Chapter IV

For patriarchal religion, in addition to the works mentioned in the text
see V. Maag, 'Malkut JHWH', *SVT* 7, 1960, 129ff.; F. Weidmann, *Die
Patriarchen und ihre Religion*, 1968; W. H. Schmidt, *Alttestamentlicher
Glaube und seine Umwelt*, 1968; G. Fohrer, *History of Israelite Religion*,
SPCK 1973. For Moses, M. Noth, *Überlieferungsgeschichte des Penta-
teuch*, 1948; 172ff.; K. Koch, 'Der Tod des Religionsstifters', *KuD* 8,
1962, 100ff.; F. Baumgärtel, *KuD* 9, 1963, 223ff.; S. Herrmann, *A
History of Israel in Old Testament Times*, SCM Press 1975. For Old
Testament religion see O. Kaiser and H. H. Schmid, in *Theologie und
Religionswissenschaft*, ed. U. Mann, 1973, pp. 241ff.; esp. 269ff.

The nature of Old Testament theology is discussed in L. Köhler,
Theologie des Alten Testaments, ⁴1966; G. von Rad, *Old Testament
Theology*, vols. 1 and 2, Oliver and Boyd 1962, 1965; W. H. Schmidt,

'Theologie des AT vor und nach G. von Rad', *VuF* 17, 1972, 1ff. The most recent accounts are: W. Zimmerli, *Grundriss der Theologie des AT*, 1972; G. Fohrer, *Theologische Grundstrukturen des AT*, 1972. For wisdom see especially C. Westermann and H.-J. Hermisson, in *Probleme biblischer Theologie* (Festschrift von Rad), 1971, pp. 611ff., pp. 136ff. For hermeneutics see C. Westermann (ed.), *Essays on Old Testament Interpretation*, SCM Press 1963; H. J. Kraus, *Die biblische Theologie*, 1970.